Y0-AGJ-484

# DRED SCOTT v. SANDFORD

**ABDO**
Publishing Company

*Landmark Supreme Court Cases*

# DRED SCOTT *v.* SANDFORD

## SLAVERY AND FREEDOM BEFORE THE AMERICAN CIVIL WAR

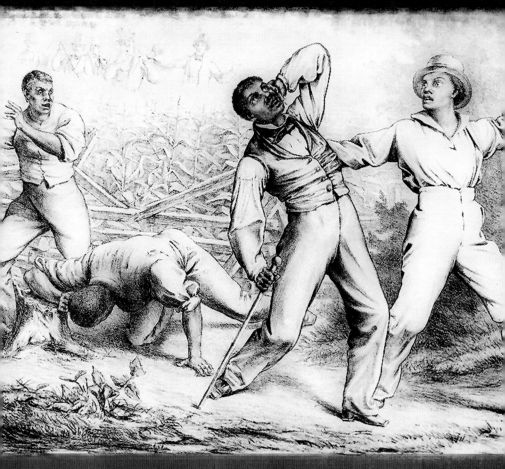

by Amy Van Zee

**Content Consultant**
Earl Maltz
Distinguished Professor
The School of Law–Camden, Rutgers University

# CREDITS

Published by ABDO Publishing Company, PO Box 398166, Minneapolis, MN 55439. Copyright © 2013 by Abdo Consulting Group, Inc. International copyrights reserved in all countries. No part of this book may be reproduced in any form without written permission from the publisher. The Essential Library™ is a trademark and logo of ABDO Publishing Company.

Printed in the United States of America,
North Mankato, Minnesota
062012
092012

Editor: Melissa York
Series Designer: Emily Love

## Library of Congress Cataloging-in-Publication Data
Van Zee, Amy.
  Dred Scott v. Sandford : slavery and freedom before the American civil war / by Amy Van Zee ; content consultant, Earl Maltz.
     p. cm. -- (Landmark Supreme Court cases)
  Includes bibliographical references.
  ISBN 978-1-61783-472-1
  1. Scott, Dred, 1809-1858--Trials, litigation, etc.--Juvenile literature. 2. Sanford, John F.A., 1806- or 7-1857--Trials, litigation, etc.--Juvenile literature. 3. Slavery--Law and legislation--United States--History--19th century--Juvenile literature. 4. Trial and arbitral proceedings. I. Maltz, Earl M., 1950- II. Title. III. Title: Dred Scott vs. Sandford. IV. Title: Dred Scott versus Sandford.
  KF228.S27V36 2013
  342.7308'7--dc23
                                    2012001276

## Photo Credits

Louis Schultze/Missouri History Museum, St. Louis, cover; Library of Congress, 9, 45, 50, 62, 72, 90, 105, 109, 118; N. Currier/Library of Congress, 14; North Wind Picture Archives, 19, 35, 41, 53; Junius Brutus Stearns/Library of Congress, 27; Bettmann/Corbis/AP Images, 33, 94; Henry Lewis/Minnesota Historical Society, 67; Th. Kaufmann/Library of Congress, 3, 81; Calvin Jackson/Library of Congress, 122; King & Baird/Library of Congress, 127; Jeff Roberson/AP Images, 132; AP Images, 137

# Table of Contents

# WHAT IS THE US SUPREME COURT?

The US Supreme Court, located in Washington DC, is the highest court in the United States and authorized to exist by the US Constitution. It consists of a chief justice and eight associate justices nominated by the president of the United States and approved by the US Senate. The justices are appointed to serve for life. A term of the court is from the first Monday in October to the first Monday in October the following year.

Each year, the justices are asked to consider more than 7,000 cases. They vote on which petitions they will grant. Four of the nine justices must vote in favor of granting a petition before a case moves forward. Currently, the justices decide between 100 and 150 cases per term.

The justices generally choose cases that address questions of state or federal laws or other constitutional questions they have not previously ruled on. The Supreme Court cannot simply declare a law unconstitutional; it must wait until someone appeals a lower court's ruling on the law.

# HOW DOES THE APPEALS PROCESS WORK?

A case usually begins in a local court. For a case involving a federal law, this is usually a federal district court. For a case involving a state or local law, this is a local trial court.

If a defendant is found guilty in a criminal trial and believes the trial court made an error, that person may appeal the case to a higher court. The defendant, now called an appellant, files a brief that explains the error the trial court allegedly made and asks for the decision to be reversed.

An appellate court, or court of appeals, reviews the records of the lower court but does not look at other evidence or call witnesses. If the appeals court finds no errors were made, the appellant may go one step further and petition the US Supreme Court to review the case. A case ruled on in a state's highest court may be appealed to the US Supreme Court.

A Supreme Court decision is based on a majority vote. Occasionally one or more justices will abstain from a case, however, a majority vote by the remaining justices is still needed to overturn a lower-court ruling. What the US Supreme Court decides is final; there is no other court to which a person can appeal. In addition, these rulings set precedent for future rulings. Unless the circumstances are greatly changed, the Supreme Court makes rulings that are consistent with its past decisions. Only an amendment to the US Constitution can overturn a Supreme Court ruling.

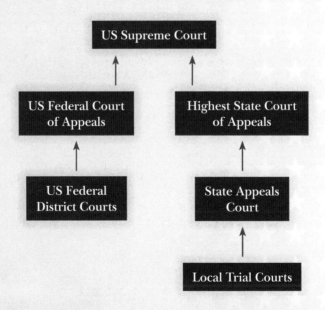

# Chapter 1

# The Decision Announced

On March 6, 1857, journalists and spectators gathered in a courtroom inside the US Capitol in Washington DC. In a few moments, a Supreme Court ruling would decide the fate of Dred Scott, a slave who had sued for his freedom in 1846. Usually the courtrooms were relatively quiet when an opinion was delivered, but this was no small case. A few months earlier, a *New York Times* journalist had reported, "The case is a peculiar one. . . . the decision will be looked for with great interest."[1] The reporter's prediction proved correct, for on this day, the courtroom was buzzing with anticipation.

Dred Scott as drawn for a nineteenth-century newspaper

Scott's original suit for freedom was against Irene Emerson, the widow of his owner. She moved out of Missouri, remarried in 1850, and passed on her legal responsibilities to her brother, John Sanford. The case name *Scott v. Sandford* includes a misspelling of the defendant's name. Sanford's name was spelled incorrectly in the Supreme Court report, and it was never corrected.

The **plaintiff**, Scott, was not in attendance on that Friday morning. More than a decade after beginning legal action for freedom, Scott was living as a slave in Saint Louis, Missouri. The **defendant**, John F. A. Sanford, was also missing from the courtroom that day. Sanford was the brother of Eliza Irene Emerson, Scott's owner at the time Scott originally sued for his freedom. When the Supreme Court's ruling was delivered, Sanford was living in an insane asylum.

## The *Scott* Case

When Scott first brought his case before a Missouri court in 1846, he was simply suing for his freedom—and chances were good he would win. Scott's owner had brought him to live in free territories, and Scott believed this should make him a free man. At the time, this case was not unique, and

Missouri courts had consistently ruled in favor of slaves in cases such as Scott's. But complexities in the case—and a persistent defendant—made the case drag on.

Over the 11-year period in which it traveled through the court systems, the *Scott* case raised new questions that begged for answers. Ultimately, the Supreme Court's ruling would make a statement not only about Scott's enslavement, but also about blacks' citizenship in the United States, their right to **sue** in federal court, the nature of enslaved people as property, and the power of Congress and the Supreme Court. Instead of merely resolving the question of Scott's freedom, the court was attempting to resolve these larger issues once and for all.

## The Issue Explodes While the Court Decides

After years of legal proceedings in the lower courts, Scott **appealed** to the Supreme Court in December 1854. But

**appealed**—Petitioned a higher court to review the decision or proceedings of a lower court.

**defendant**—The person against whom legal action is brought.

**plaintiff**—A person or group of people who bring legal action against another person, group, or organization.

**sue**—To bring legal action against.

it was not until February 1856 that the court heard the case for the first time. After delays and more arguments in December, the court postponed its decision until early 1857. This delay would be incredibly significant in the case, for while the *Scott* case sat in the Supreme Court, the nation's stance on slavery was shifting. A few

## THE US COURT SYSTEM

The US judiciary is made up of the federal court system and the state court system, which often interact. The Constitution provides the federal government with specific powers, and, unless explicitly prohibited, the remaining powers fall to the states. Therefore, the separate systems are needed, because state and federal laws and powers are unique. The area in which each court can rule is referred to as its jurisdiction.

Scott's legal battle took him through both the state court system and the federal court system. In Missouri, his case against Irene Emerson was heard twice in a state circuit court in Saint Louis. A circuit court is a court that sits in two or more places in its district. Then it traveled to the Missouri Supreme Court. Scott then began a new suit at the US Circuit Court for Missouri. This case was under federal jurisdiction because Scott, who filed as a Missouri citizen, brought a suit against Sanford, a New York citizen, and federal courts have jurisdiction when a case involves parties from different states. The case then traveled to the US Supreme Court for its final decision. Today, the Supreme Court decides which cases it wishes to review. At the time of the *Scott* case, however, the Supreme Court heard every case that came before it.

key events that took place during this time ensured the court's decision in the *Scott* case would be monumental.

As the United States physically expanded and settlers pushed westward, the question of extending slavery to these new territories provoked heated discussion from both sides. Much of the public eye focused on Kansas. In 1854, the Kansas-Nebraska Act passed through Congress, allowing residents of Kansas to decide for themselves whether slavery would be allowed in their territory—instead of Congress making this decision on their behalf. While this bill pleased Southerners, it outraged Northerners because it directly contradicted the Missouri Compromise of 1820, which declared slavery would not extend north of Missouri. Kansas became a hotbed of violence as pro- and antislavery advocates flocked to the territory to fight for their beliefs and to influence the territory in deciding whether to allow slavery. Approximately 55 people died during the massacres and riots that became known as Bleeding Kansas.

In the midst of this turmoil, the nation elected a new president. At that time, political parties were in many ways defined by their stance on slavery and whether Congress had the constitutional right to prohibit it, and the election of 1856 centered on this topic.

President Buchanan would prove unable to heal the country's growing rift over slavery.

James Buchanan ran as the presidential candidate for the Democratic Party. His party endorsed the policy of popular sovereignty, which meant territories could decide for themselves whether to allow or forbid slavery. The Republican Party and its candidate, John C. Frémont, believed Congress had the right and duty to prohibit slavery in the territories. Former president

Millard Fillmore ran as the nominee for the American Party, or Know-Nothing Party. The group was split on the issue of slavery, but it focused on the need for compromise. Although Buchanan failed to win the popular majority in the three-way race, he won sufficient electoral votes to become the fifteenth president of the United States. He was inaugurated on March 4, 1857, just two days before the decision was announced in the *Scott* case.

## The Weight of the Case

Although the *Scott* case was on hold while violence raged in Kansas and the nation elected a new president, the case did not fade from the public's view. Instead, its notoriety only grew. US citizens waited anxiously for the court's ruling in early March. In his inaugural address, President Buchanan hinted at the decision that would be made by the Supreme Court. He stated, "To their decision, in common with all good citizens, I shall cheerfully submit, whatever this may be."[2]

The people involved in the case knew the considerable weight the decision would carry. Montgomery Blair, the lawyer who acted on behalf of Scott, discussed Congress's right to prohibit slavery in the territories during his statements before the Supreme Court. On this subject, he declared,

> *This is a question of more importance, perhaps, than any which was ever submitted to this court; and the decision of the court is looked for with a degree of interest by the country which seldom attends its proceedings. It is, indeed, the great question of our day and times, and is, substantially, the issue on which the great political divisions among men is founded in all times and countries.*[3]

But just what that decision would be was unknown. Would the Supreme Court rule in favor of Scott and his family and declare them free? Or would the court strike down the case and declare that blacks could not sue? Would slavery stand in the territories? And who had the power to decide this—the people or Congress?

Dressed in black, the nine **justices** entered the courtroom at 11:00 a.m. on March 6 to deliver their opinion to the waiting crowd. **Chief Justice** Roger B. Taney would deliver the ruling. Stooped and feeble, the 79-year-old Taney carefully read the opinion. The

**chief justice**—The presiding judge of the US Supreme Court.

**justice**—A member of the US Supreme Court.

document was 55 pages long and the speech lasted two hours. The men and women in attendance listened with intense interest, for they knew the *Scott* decision would affect more than just the Missouri slave and his family. Indeed, the *Scott* decision would become one of the events leading to a long and bloody civil war and, ultimately, the abolition of slavery in the United States. ∼

# Chapter 2

# Slavery in the New World

By the 1840s, when the *Scott* case was first beginning, slavery already had deep roots in the United States—especially in the South. The ownership of humans had begun in the New World in some of the earliest colonial settlements, and it was ingrained in the American way of life.

In the early seventeenth century, English colonists in the Virginia settlement learned to grow tobacco, and the crop became an important source of revenue. However, growing tobacco required a great deal of human labor. In response to this demand, many Europeans came to the New World as indentured servants. These servants—who were

African slaves were introduced to the Jamestown settlement in the early seventeenth century.

usually white—sold themselves into a sort of slavery in exchange for transport to North America. Many left their homeland in search of a better life, and their temporary slavery was a means to this end. They were

## THE MIDDLE PASSAGE

Captive Africans endured long voyages across the Atlantic to the New World. They were often chained together below the main deck of the ship. The hot, crowded conditions caused some to resort to suicide if they had a chance to jump overboard, and the mortality rate during the Middle Passage was estimated to be at least 15 percent.[2] After learning of the horrible conditions aboard slave ships, abolitionists made this information public to help further their cause.

free after they had paid off their debt, which usually took between four and seven years.

In contrast to indentured servants, black slaves did not come voluntarily. On August 20, 1619, a Dutch ship brought the first captive Africans to the English colony of Jamestown in North America. These first captive Africans were indentured servants, but slavery eventually became permanent for Africans and their descendants. By 1649, 300 blacks lived in Virginia, and the idea of black slavery had taken hold because blacks were seen as inferior to whites.[1] Historian Don E. Fehrenbacher notes that the institution and rationalization of black slavery caught on swiftly in the colonies, in part because English colonists had watched the Spanish and Portuguese enslave blacks for more than 100 years.

## Slavery and the Law

Legally, both indentured servants and black slaves were considered property—they could be bought, sold, and inherited by their owner's children. The first laws that governed these people as property applied to indentured servants, but the laws and the courts would soon differentiate between indentured servant and slave. For example, in 1640, a Virginia court ruling took race into account when issuing **sentences** in *Re Negro John Punch*. Three servants, two white and one black, ran away from their master. In addition to a whipping, the two white servants were sentenced to four years of additional enslavement. The black servant was whipped and sentenced to life enslavement.

In the 1660s, as the number of African slaves grew, the colonies began enacting laws pertaining specifically to slavery. For example, in 1662, a Virginia law declared slavery to be lifelong, and eventually, the rest of the colonies declared the same. Additionally, children born of slaves—including the child of a slave mother and a white master—were slaves belonging solely to the

**sentence**—A decision by a judge or court including the punishment for the person convicted.

master. This differed from English law, in which children adopted the same status as their father. By fathering children with their own slaves, white masters could essentially breed a new generation of slaves. Slaves had to obey their masters, and any work made by the slave belonged to the master. All of these laws reinforced the idea that slaves were property.

But other laws and beliefs contradicted the concept of slaves as property. For example, slaves were regarded as people in criminal cases, in which the slaves were held personally responsible for any wrongdoing. Additionally, many slaveholders believed slavery was a means of civilizing black people, which further acknowledged that blacks were more than just property. These warring ideas,

## INTERRACIAL RELATIONSHIPS

It was common for white masters to sexually exploit their female slaves. Slaves who worked in homes were especially at risk. Although this practice was socially accepted, both Northern and Southern colonies passed laws that discouraged interracial marriage. In 1664, Maryland passed a law stating that any white woman marrying a black man could become a slave herself. In the late seventeenth century, Virginia banned interracial marriages, and Massachusetts did the same in 1705.

that slaves were both people and property, highlighted the basic contradiction in slave laws.

Generally, slave codes in the Northern and middle colonies varied from Southern laws, in part because the use of slaves varied from North to South. Although tobacco plantations in Rhode Island made use of slaves as field hands, black slaves in the North often worked in homes as domestic servants. In 1750, Rhode Island was the only New England colony with a slave population of more than 10 percent. In contrast, the population of South Carolina was 70 percent slaves in 1720.[3] Estimates show that black slaves made up approximately 40 percent of the total Southern population at the time of the American Revolution (1775–1784).[4] Many Southern plantation owners relied heavily upon unpaid black labor for planting and crop harvesting. In the South, as the populations of blacks grew quickly, Southern laws became more restrictive. These laws forbade slaves from owning property, obtaining legally recognized marriages, and **testifying** against whites in court.

**testifying**—Declaring something in court under oath.

# Fighting for Freedom

In the 1760s, tensions were increasing between Great Britain and the 13 North American colonies. In the first half of that century, Britain had been engaged in wars that distracted the nation and allowed the colonies a greater degree of freedom. But the wars had drained Britain financially, and the country needed to raise money. To do so, Britain increased its taxation in the colonies and passed laws tightening its control over them. The colonists resented these actions and the increased British military presence, which they interpreted as violations of their liberty. Many responded with acts of **civil disobedience**, claiming their right to self-government. In 1775, the Revolutionary War broke out. On July 2, 1776, the Continental Congress agreed to split from Britain. A few days later, on July 4, the Congress adopted the Declaration of Independence. It stated, "We hold these truths to be self-evident, that all men are created equal."[5]

Throughout the American Revolution, the metaphor of slavery was used to attack Britain's grasp on

---

**civil disobedience**—A refusal to obey the government or laws in order to protest government action.

## BLACKS AND THE REVOLUTIONARY WAR

Not all American slaves who fought in the Revolutionary War fought on behalf of the colonies. Some believed that working with the British would offer a better chance for freedom. In 1775, a British loyalist in Virginia offered freedom to any slave or servant who fought for the British, and slaves responded enthusiastically to the call to join the British forces.

As a result, the colonists began recruiting blacks. Some Northern colonies, including Rhode Island, New Hampshire, and New Jersey, offered freedom to blacks who served in the state militia, and Congress began pushing Southern states to do the same. Southerners were unwilling to give up their slaves or allow them access to guns. Most Southern militias did not include blacks, despite the need for troops. At the end of the war, more than 5,000 blacks had served in the American forces.[6]

the American colonies. Revolutionaries such as Samuel Adams and George Washington criticized Britain and its king for treating the colonists as slaves. But their antislavery contemporaries were quick to point out their hypocrisy, for in the colonies, the enslavement of blacks remained. One author wrote,

> *Blush ye pretended votaries for freedom! ye trifling patriots! . . . for while you are fasting, praying, . . . remonstrating, resolving, and pleading*

*for a restoration of your charter rights, you at the same time are continuing this lawless, cruel, inhuman, and abominable practice of enslaving your fellow men.*[7]

Around this time, a passionate antislavery faction began forming, mostly in the North. Antislavery groups included both whites and blacks who used the declaration of freedom from Britain as the basis that freedom should be for all people. At the time, many of those who supported slavery argued that blacks were barbarians, and it was the white man's Christian duty to help civilize blacks through slavery. But antislavery groups such as the Quakers began attacking this belief directly by declaring that slavery and Christianity could not coexist. Enslaved blacks who protested their slavery used Christian language to make their plea, stating "We desire to bless God, who loves Mankind."[8]

## Slavery and the Drafting of the Constitution

Many blacks participated in the American Revolution through protests and military service, but the war did not result in the national abolition of slavery. After a peace treaty between the United States and Britain

George Washington with his slaves

was ratified in 1784, the United States became an independent nation. In May 1787, a Constitutional Convention began with the goal of revising the Articles of Confederation, which had loosely governed the states since 1781. The articles bound the states together in a confederation, but many, including James Madison, saw the articles as weak because they did not establish a central government above the states. Therefore, resolving national issues was extremely difficult.

At the Constitutional Convention, the delegates realized they needed an entirely new plan of government, replacing the old Articles of Confederation. At the time of the convention, views of slavery created sharp geographic divisions. These divisions ran so deep they threatened the unity of the new nation. The issue of slavery would arise in unexpected places—from the power of each state's electors to each state's duty to recognize the laws of another state—as the men in attendance debated the form the new central government should take. The delegates found slavery so entwined in the issues they faced that it could not be ignored. Slavery would play a large role in two important topics for debate at the convention, even though the word *slavery* did not appear in the original Constitution.

First, slavery came up for debate when determining how the **legislature** should be organized and how many members it would have. After much debate, the delegates resolved on the two legislative houses: one house would have equal representation from each state, the other representation based on population. But how would this population be determined? Would slaves count toward the population of each state? Southerners argued yes, hoping their large slave populations would earn them greater representation in the new government. Northerners argued no, stating Southerners claimed black slaves as property rather than citizens, so therefore

**legislature**—An official body that makes laws.

## WHY SLAVERY?

Before the American Civil War (1861–1865) violently ended the practice of slavery in the United States, slavery was one of the foundations of society in the South. Slavery was a central part of the economy. Slavery allowed the massive cotton plantations to be profitable after the 1793 invention of the cotton gin, a machine that quickly separated cotton fibers from the seeds. The introduction of cloth mills run by steam engines allowed industry in the North to keep up with the South's increased supply of cotton. Thus slavery was woven into the economy of the entire country, not just the South.

The economic pressures of slavery coupled with social pressures to entrench the practice. Most whites, North and South, believed blacks were inferior. Some even believed blacks were not fully human. Indeed, many slave owners believed slavery was good for society because it kept blacks in their place and allowed whites to civilize and Christianize them. Increasingly throughout the nineteenth century, however, religion inspired abolitionists to take up the antislavery cause.

slaves could not count toward a state's population. The delegates compromised by deciding that populations would count free persons and "three fifths of all other Persons," another way of saying slaves.[9] Known as the Three-Fifths Compromise and referred to as the Three-Fifths Clause in the Constitution, this count also applied to taxation. So although counting three-fifths of slaves in the populations would give slaveholding states more representatives in Congress, white residents would also pay additional taxes for their slaves. The language appears in Article I, Section 2 of the Constitution. From its very beginning, the document favored those who owned slaves.

The second way in which slavery divided delegates was in discussions regarding the slave trade. The issue was whether states could decide for themselves if they wanted to allow or prohibit the slave trade. Even the South was divided. Georgia, North Carolina, and South Carolina were in favor of each state deciding this issue for itself, but Virginia wanted the slave trade ended. Ultimately, the language of the slave-trade clause reflected the compromise reached: Congress would not make a law to prohibit the slave trade before 1808.

Through many debates, the delegates carefully avoided specific mention of slavery in the Constitution. But one clause, the fugitive-slave clause, would later be interpreted as **constitutional** protection for slavery. It stated,

**constitutional**—In accordance with a constitution.

*No person held to service or labor in one state, under the laws thereof, escaping into another, shall, in consequence of any law or regulation therein, be discharged from such service or labor, but shall be delivered up on claim of the party to whom such service or labor may be due.*[10]

In other words, the law said a fugitive slave who escaped from one state to another should be returned. At the Convention, the fugitive-slave clause did not stir the delegates to much debate and it passed unanimously. But in practice this clause was problematic, for in returning a fugitive slave, a free state was submitting to the laws of a slave state. This clause was the basis of future legislation and future quarreling.

The delegates signed the Constitution on September 17, 1787. During the convention, the delegates learned slavery could be a very useful bargaining tool—both for the North and for the South. Further compromises between slave and free states would be needed as the nation acquired western territories and expanded. ~

The Constitution's compromises about slavery
would not last long.

# Chapter 3

# The Territorial Question

When slavery entered into the debates at the Constitutional Convention, the delegates at the convention largely concerned themselves with the states that already existed. But questions quickly arose about whether slavery would expand into the new territories west of the existing states—and who should decide the slavery question in these regions. While the delegates to the Constitutional Convention were debating the structure of a new federal government in Philadelphia, the Continental Congress in New York was debating the future of slavery in new territories.

On July 13, 1787, Congress passed the Northwest Ordinance. The Northwest Ordinance

The land organized by the Northwest Ordinance was known as the Northwest Territory.

was a piece of federal legislation that addressed the issues of governance in new territories that existed west of Pennsylvania, north of the Ohio River, and east of the Mississippi River. This land makes up the present-day states of Ohio, Indiana, Illinois, Michigan, Wisconsin, and part of Minnesota. The ordinance outlined a process by which a territory, as its population grew, could appoint officials who would speak in Washington DC on behalf of the territory. When the adult male population in a territory grew large enough—to 60,000 residents—the territory could take steps to apply for statehood and self-government. In addition, the Northwest Ordinance banned slavery in these new territories. The eight states present at Congress, five of which were Southern states, unanimously passed the ordinance. As president, George Washington signed the legislation.

There are a number of reasons why the Southern states passed legislation that appeared to be so antislavery. First, by explicitly forbidding slavery in the Northwest, the ordinance was implying that slavery was legal in the Southwest. Next, the Northwest Ordinance contained language that protected the rights of one state's people to pursue and capture escaped slaves who

## NORTHWEST ORDINANCE AND THE CONSTITUTIONAL CONVENTION

The Northwest Ordinance was passed at the same time members of the Constitutional Convention were discussing how to count slave populations toward representation and taxation. Delegates at the convention likely knew about the almost final decision to pass the Northwest Ordinance. The new legislation may have come to bear upon their decisions, making proslavery delegates more willing to compromise because of their approval of the Northwest Ordinance.

fled to the free territories. This appealed to the Southern states' desire for state sovereignty in relation to slavery. And finally, some Southerners might have supported the abolition of slavery in the Northwest for economic reasons. Cheap slave labor in the Northwest would create competition for the Southern plantations.

Additionally, the passing of the Northwest Ordinance brought up the question of whether Congress even had the constitutional power to pass such legislation. At the time, no protests arose about Congress's power to forbid slavery in the territories. And in 1789, when Congress reenacted the Northwest Ordinance, Congress included 19 delegates who had attended the Constitutional Convention. These men were familiar with the Constitution and the powers contained within it. Later, the issue of whether Congress had the power to legislate slavery in the territories would weigh heavily in the *Scott* case.

In 1790, Congress organized the Southwest Territory (the future state of Tennessee) in a manner similar to the Northwest Territory, but without a ban on slavery. In this region, slavery existed because of congressional silence on the topic, not because of explicit congressional allowance. Whether to allow or forbid slavery was essentially left to the people in the region. This was an early example of congressional nonintervention and popular sovereignty. Slavery could exist anywhere if the law did not explicitly forbid it. The organization of the Southwest without antislavery legislation continued to split the country geographically into a proslavery South and an antislavery North. Further compromises about slavery would follow this pattern of geographic division.

## Governing New Lands

President Thomas Jefferson made the Louisiana Purchase in 1803, buying more than 800,000 square miles (2,071,990 sq km) of land from France.[1] The territory was west of the Mississippi River. If Congress did not explicitly prohibit slavery in this region, it would become slave territory. The Senate debated limiting slavery in this region, with legislators offering options such as limiting the slave importation to the area. The final bill contained no restriction of slavery, but it did not authorize it either. This was another example of nonintervention. The silence was an implied consent for slavery in Louisiana Territory, which became known as Missouri Territory in 1812 after Louisiana became a state.

Ending the slave trade in 1808 had neither stopped slavery nor quieted the issue. In 1817, the United States consisted of 22 states—11 free and 11 slave states. At times, the balance had been upset on one side, but the addition of a state on the other side quickly evened the count. In this area east of the Mississippi River, the Ohio River was a clear line delineating slave states from free

## THE LOUISIANA PURCHASE

The Louisiana Purchase doubled the size of the United States. Land from the purchase makes up all or part of the modern states of Arkansas, Colorado, Iowa, Kansas, Louisiana, Minnesota, Missouri, Montana, Nebraska, New Mexico, North Dakota, Oklahoma, South Dakota, Texas, and Wyoming.

states. In 1818, a balance existed between the number of slave and free states, but that year, Missouri threatened to upset that balance by applying to enter the Union with no restriction on slavery. The Ohio River, which had served as a dividing line, cut through the middle of the state.

At this time, a great congressional debate arose about the admission of Missouri into the Union. Legislator James Tallmadge of New York proposed amendments that would limit slavery in Missouri, but this bill did not pass both houses. Meanwhile, Maine applied for admission to the Union and would become a bargaining tool for Southerners. The Senate proposed that Maine be admitted as a free state only if Missouri would be admitted as a slave state. In the compromise bills that eventually passed in March 1820, Maine was admitted as a free state. Missouri was allowed to form a state constitution, a step toward becoming a state. The agreement was reached that—with the exception of Missouri—slavery would be prohibited in the Missouri Territory north of the 36° 30' parallel, or the southern border of the state of Missouri. The next year, 1821, the state of Missouri was admitted to the Union. Its constitution allowed slavery. Although it settled tensions for the time being, the Missouri Compromise of 1820

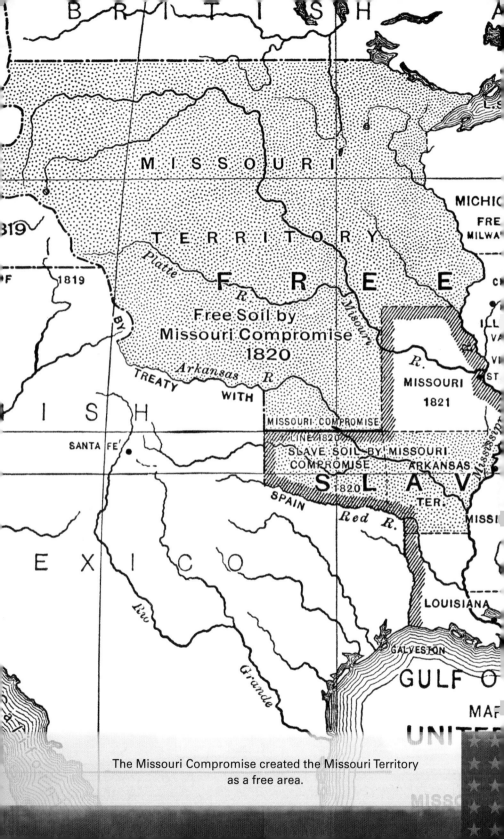

The Missouri Compromise created the Missouri Territory as a free area.

proved to be a short-lived solution to a problem that would continue to plague the United States.

## Legislation and Precedent

On February 12, 1793, President George Washington had signed the Fugitive Slave Act into law. Expanding upon the fugitive-slave clause in the Constitution, the law addressed issues of criminal **extradition**, specifically between free and slave states. If a slave fled from a slave state to a free state, the law asked the governor of the free state to return the slave to his or her master. The law also allowed a slave hunter to cross the state line to pursue a fugitive slave. Upon finding the slave, if the slave hunter showed a judge or magistrate proof of ownership, the slave hunter could take the slave back to the slave state. Anyone who aided a fugitive could be fined $500.

The Fugitive Slave Act had wide implications. In attempting to deal with the problems of state relations regarding slavery, the act became a federal law that ignored state sovereignty. With no time limit specified, a fugitive slave could be captured years after escape, and a captured slave was not entitled to a trial by **jury**. Free blacks were at risk for abuse of this law, especially in the South. In response, many Northern

## THE *AMISTAD* CASE

As federal laws relating to slavery passed, the judiciary was also making statements from the bench. One famous case went all the way to the Supreme Court. In 1839, a group of African slaves aboard *La Amistad* took control of the slave ship as it was traveling to Cuba. They killed many of the white crew and eventually landed in New York, where they were tried for mutiny. But the Africans had been captured illegally, and the Supreme Court ruled in favor of their freedom. The captives who survived returned to Africa in 1842.

The case is a landmark because, at the time, the rights of blacks were not well defended. Former US president John Quincy Adams acted as one of the chief lawyers on behalf of the Africans. The ruling in favor of the Africans was regarded as a victory for the abolitionist cause.

states passed personal liberty laws that protected freed or escaped blacks through jury trials. Some even forbade compliance with this federal law. This worsened the issue and angered Southerners.

**extradition**—The transfer of an alleged criminal from one authority to another for trial.

**jury**—A group of people selected to deliver a verdict on an issue, such as a court case.

An 1842 Supreme Court ruling addressed this very issue. In *Prigg v. Pennsylvania*, the Supreme Court ruled that these state fugitive slave laws were **unconstitutional** because the higher federal law provided for the return of captured slaves. In this particular case, a slave catcher, Edward Prigg, had captured escaped slave Margaret Morgan in Pennsylvania. He asked a local magistrate to return her and her two children to Maryland. The judge refused to issue the certificates needed to do so legally, and Prigg removed Morgan and her family illegally to Maryland. Prigg was charged by Pennsylvania for kidnapping, and he appealed to the Supreme Court.

The court reversed the decision and sided with Prigg. The court's decision, written by Justice Joseph

## THE FREE SOIL PARTY

There were many reasons for opposing slavery. The Free Soil Party, which was organized in 1848, held the motto "free soil, free speech, free labor, free men."[2] The party opposed the spread of slavery into new US territories, but its reasoning had an economic basis. Members of the Free Soil Party feared they would not be able to compete with free slave labor if it continued to expand westward. So while the party tended to be antislavery, it still maintained that blacks were inferior to whites and did not generally support abolition.

Justice Story often ruled in ways that limited slavery.

Story, declared the Pennsylvania laws unconstitutional
because they contradicted the fugitive-slave clause of
the Constitution. Story emphasized that the Fugitive
Slave Act was authorized by the fugitive-slave clause

**unconstitutional**—Inconsistent with a constitution.

## STATE AND FEDERAL RIGHTS

The US government is structured under federalism, a system defined by the sharing of powers between the central, federal government and the individual states. Constitutionally, certain powers are given explicitly to the federal government, including foreign trade and the right to declare war. The states can claim powers that are not given to the federal government and that are not explicitly denied them. These powers include education and family issues such as marriage and divorce.

While the Constitutional Convention was at work, a group named the Anti-Federalists opposed the Constitution because they believed it gave too much power to the central government and robbed the states of their individual sovereignty. At the time, the states were used to exercising a great deal of control over themselves, including writing legislation about slavery and other issues. The creation of the federal government created a tension between states' rights and federal power that still exists today. This tension can be seen in current debate about issues such as health care and marijuana legislation.

in the Constitution, making the issue a federal one. He interpreted the federal laws to give anyone the right to cross state lines to recapture a slave, and stated the federal government was responsible for enforcing the law, not the states. In the landmark decision, the Supreme Court acknowledged that slavery was part of the Constitution, that there was federal protection for slavery, and that slavery was not just a state issue. The decision also implied slaves were property to be recovered, which pleased Southerners.

But by making slave recapture and the enforcement of the fugitive slave law a federal issue, the states' powers were weakened on these issues. Taking advantage of slave recovery as a federal responsibility, some Northern states passed laws prohibiting their state officials from helping recover a runaway slave. Recognizing this, some Southern states began pushing for stronger, and more explicit, federal legislation in favor of slaveholders' rights. However, other Southerners were against federal legislation because they feared making slavery a federal issue would give the federal government the power to abolish slavery in the future. In general, both Southern and Northern views of whether slavery should be regulated on a federal level shifted whenever it could be favorable to their faction. Soon, the *Scott* case would worsen these tensions between state power and federal power and between North and South. ～

# Chapter 4

# Slaves, Freedom, and Civil Rights

Even if a person was born into slavery, it was possible for him or her to become free. One way to become free was to escape to states where slavery was outlawed. In 1777, Vermont abolished slavery. By 1804, the rest of the Northern states had done the same, although the abolition provided for was often gradual, meaning slaves were freed after they had worked for a number of years or had reached a certain age. Many Southern slaves, including famous abolitionist Frederick Douglass, escaped and traveled North to freedom.

Often a slave attempted to escape because of a traumatic event. After an incident of heavy physical

## FREDERICK DOUGLASS

Frederick Augustus Washington Bailey was born in 1818 to a slave woman and a white man. Enslaved and often brutally whipped, Frederick nonetheless learned to read when he was eight years old. In 1836, he intended to escape, but his plans were discovered and he was sent to jail. In 1838, he fled to freedom, settling in Massachusetts and changing his name to Frederick Douglass. After meeting abolitionist William Lloyd Garrison, Douglass joined the cause, giving lectures about his experiences as a slave and publishing his first autobiography, *Narrative of the Life of Frederick Douglass,* in 1845. In 1848, he published the first issue of the *North Star*, his abolitionist newspaper. During the Civil War, he discussed slavery with President Abraham Lincoln. Douglass died in 1895.

abuse or facing the sale of one's family, a desperate slave might decide to run away. However, traveling with a family was incredibly difficult, as escape often involved little food alongside exposure to harsh weather and terrain. Most runaway slaves were single young men. Mothers traveling with children rarely reached freedom.

## Manumission

But slaves could also acquire freedom through other means. One way was through manumission, in which a slave owner intentionally emancipated a slave. A slave

Slaves who were not manumitted could try to
escape to free lands.

might be manumitted for good behavior or through purchasing freedom from the owner. A slave also might be set free in a master's will. Most manumissions were for individual slaves or families, but some larger manumission events occurred. For example, in 1808, Virginian Samuel Gist wrote in his will that all 274 of his slaves would be emancipated upon his death.[1] This emancipation was one of the largest in the state of Virginia.

However, free blacks posed a threat to the slaveholding Southern states. Slave owners feared free blacks would stir up slaves to revolt and rebel. Throughout the history of the colonies, local laws had placed heavy restrictions on the freeing of blacks. For example, a Virginia law in the seventeenth century required any slave owner who freed a slave to pay for the slave to leave the colony. Later colonial laws stipulated that if a slave did not leave the colony within six or 12 months, he could be re-enslaved. These laws were relaxed during the American Revolution, but many were reinstated after large slave revolts occurred in the early nineteenth century. Some states passed laws prohibiting manumission through wills, while others stopped the practice of allowing slaves to hire out their free time to earn money to purchase their freedom.

Manumission struck deeply against the slaveholding ideology. In this ideology, slavery was part of the foundation of society; it kept everyone in their correct social place, and it was a means to civilize and Christianize blacks. To manumit a slave was to proclaim something was wrong with the institution of slavery, to say blacks were better off free. In this way, whenever a slave sought his or her freedom, Southerners saw it as an attack on their society and their way of life. This tension

## NAT TURNER'S REVOLT

Nat Turner, born a slave in 1800 in Virginia, led the only successful large-scale slave rebellion in the United States. Turner believed he was called by God to lead his people out of slavery. Beginning on August 21, 1831, Turner and his followers killed his owners and approximately 60 white people. Soldiers put down the rebellion before Turner reached the nearby armory where weapons were stored. The soldiers and mobs of angry whites killed many innocent blacks in the process. Turner fled and hid, but he was found six weeks later and executed.

Before Turner's rebellion, Southern slave owners believed blacks were satisfied with slavery or were too oppressed to rebel. After, Southern whites' fear of slave rebellions grew, and new laws in many areas restricted blacks more than before.

The reality of slave rebellions such as Nat Turner's conflicted with the Southern belief that slavery was good for blacks.

also underlay the *Scott* case. For Scott to even want to be free became an attack on the institution of slavery.

## Freedom through the Courts

Legally, complications arose when a slave owner moved between slave and free states or territories. For example, if a master and a slave traveled from a slave state to a free state, was the slave freed upon entering free soil where slavery is prohibited? What if the slave returned to a state that allowed slavery? These questions became important issues as state governments struggled to accommodate the laws of other states, especially because there was no federal law banning slavery.

Three general answers were applied to these questions. First, some believed a law governing the status of a slave essentially traveled with the slave. Therefore, a slave's status would not change as the slave moved from state to state. Second, others believed a slave should be declared free upon moving to a free state, and, once this slave was free, he was free forever. And third, yet others believed that, upon moving to a free state, the slave was free from his owner's control, but, upon moving back to a slave state, the owner's control returned. This was the principle of reattachment.

These differing views caused much trouble when a slave brought a suit for freedom, for even the Constitution provided for the return of fugitive slaves to their respective states. This principle, called reversion, meant courts had to decide which state's laws would be upheld—would the free state's laws be applied to the slave returning to the slave state? Or would the

## HARRIET TUBMAN AND THE UNDERGROUND RAILROAD

Born a slave in Maryland around 1820, Harriet Tubman escaped in 1849 after enduring years of physical abuse. Arriving in Philadelphia, Pennsylvania, she was able to find work. But instead of staying in the free North, Tubman returned to the South to help her family escape. Along with her family, she helped other black slaves find their way to freedom through the Underground Railroad, a system of safe houses for escaping slaves. Tubman was seen as such a threat that, by 1856, a $40,000 bounty was put on her head. Tubman died in 1913.

slave state's laws override those of the free state? These questions remained until the Supreme Court used the *Scott* case to rule on these issues.

In determining the legal status of a slave, courts often took into account how long the slave stayed in the free state or territory. The distinction was usually made between traveling through a free state and residing or setting up a home in a free state. In general, Southern courts recognized that when a master moved to a free state to live there, his slaves were to be emancipated. Overall, the courts upheld the idea that a slave's status stayed with him or her as he or she traveled through a free state if it was only for a short period. They also upheld the principle that if a slave were emancipated through living in a free state, the slave status did not return if he or she moved back to the slave state. This followed the ruling in the English case *Somerset v. Stewart* (1772), which set a **precedent** for a slave to be freed when taken to live in a place without explicit proslavery laws. The chief justice, Lord Mansfield, declared that in cases such as these, the slave reverted to his or her natural state: free. This English decision had a lasting effect in the US legal system.

More than 50 years later, the English courts handed down another decision that would affect US courts, especially in relation to the *Scott* case. In *The Slave, Grace* (1827), the English courts ruled about the reattachment of slave laws. A slave had traveled from Antigua to England for one year with her master. After returning to Antigua, she sued for her freedom. The English court ruled that because the slave returned to a slave **jurisdiction**, the English laws of freedom no longer applied to her and she was again a slave. At the time

**jurisdiction**—The authority to govern or try cases; also refers to the territory under that authority.

**precedent**—A court ruling or decision that becomes an example and is noted in later rulings in similar cases.

Scott sued for his freedom, the Missouri courts did not follow this precedent. They ruled in favor of freedom for slaves who had lived in the North and returned to the slave state of Missouri. From 1824 to 1838, the Missouri Supreme Court heard more than ten cases from slaves suing for freedom on the basis that they had lived or worked in free states. In each one, the court ruled in favor of freedom.

## Freedom, Rights, and Citizenship

But even if a slave did acquire freedom—either through escape, manumission, or through the court system—he still faced many difficulties. First, even living in a free state, free blacks were at risk of being kidnapped and sold into slavery. In the South, blacks could not sit on a jury, testify against a white person, or move from state to state. Laws varied between the states and from North to South, but there was a general fear among whites that free blacks would cause insurrection. In Georgia, it was illegal to teach a free black to read and write. Northern states and territories such as Illinois, Indiana, and Oregon did not permit blacks to enter the state legally, though the laws were poorly enforced. On the federal level, in 1792, Congress forbade blacks from serving in the militia.

> What, to the American slave, is your 4th of July? I answer; a day that reveals to him, more than all other days in the year, the gross injustice and cruelty to which he is the constant victim. To him, your celebration is a sham; . . . your shout of liberty and equality, hollow mockery; your prayers and hymns, . . . are to him, . . . hypocrisy—a thin veil to cover up crimes which would disgrace a nation of savages. There is not a nation on the earth guilty of practices more shocking and bloody than are the people of the United States. . . ."[3]

*—FREDERICK DOUGLASS, JULY 5, 1852, SPEAKING AT AN EVENT COMMEMORATING THE FOURTH OF JULY*

Were these restrictions a violation of the rights of blacks? Article IV, Section 2 of the US Constitution declares, "The Citizens of each State shall be entitled to all Privileges and Immunities of Citizens in the several States."[2] If blacks were citizens, then these laws were unconstitutional, but not all states regarded blacks as citizens of their states. Even in the North, most blacks were denied some or all of the rights associated with citizenship today. In 1832, Roger B. Taney, who was at the time attorney general and would later rule in the *Scott* case, declared,

*The African race in the United States even when free, are everywhere a degraded class, and*

*exercise no political influence. The privileges they are allowed to enjoy, are accorded to them as a matter of kindness and benevolence rather than of right. . . . They were not looked upon as citizens by the contracting parties who formed the Constitution. They were evidently not supposed to be included by the term citizens.*[4]

Taney's words in 1832 reflected the worldview and perpetuated the idea of blacks as "others." Many whites saw blacks as beasts and grouped them with animals, and, therefore, did not regard them as human. By this logic, blacks were certainly noncitizens. This ideology was pervasive as scientists and philosophers sought to prove that blacks were inferior to whites by their very nature. In associating blacks with darkness, blacks were seen as evil, and black ancestry was a mark of being tainted and separated from what they considered the "purity" of the white race. Although some state laws and **judicial** decisions legislated or ruled about the idea of black citizenship—usually against it—the Supreme Court did not endorse or reject black citizenship until the *Scott* case. ∼

**judicial**—Relating to justice or the courts.

# Chapter 5

# Who Was Dred Scott?

laveholders did not always keep records of the births, deaths, and travels of their slaves. Much of Scott's history has been pieced together through letters and legal documents. Historians believe Scott was likely born in Virginia around the turn of the nineteenth century. He was likely called Sam for the first part of his life. Like his parents before him, Sam was the property of the Blow family.

Peter Blow and his wife Elizabeth lived in Southampton County, Virginia, with their children. The family owned and farmed 860 acres (348 ha) of land.[1] In 1818, Blow moved west to Hunstville, Alabama, and records show he took a slave named

Sam with him. The family farmed land in Alabama for 12 years before moving west again in 1830—this time to Saint Louis, Missouri, a city that was beginning to flourish as a hub of commerce and trade. Blow brought along six slaves, including Sam.

In Saint Louis, Blow tried a new profession. Instead of farming, he opened a boarding house in the bustling city and named it the Jefferson Hotel. Blow fell into debt in his new venture. His wife died in 1831, and he eventually gave up on his hotel. Blow died on June 23, 1832. Around this time, the family sold Sam, likely to help pay down debt.

Dr. John Emerson purchased a slave from the Blow family around this time. Historians believe it likely that

## SAINT LOUIS, MISSOURI

The city of Saint Louis is known as the Gateway to the West. Located on the banks of the Mississippi River, the city quickly became a popular trading post after French fur traders settled in the area in 1764. As the United States gained territory through the Louisiana Purchase, settlers often stopped at Saint Louis before traveling west. Northerners and Southerners flocked to the new boomtown, which also served as a jumping off point between east and west.

Saint Louis ca. 1850

## THE NAME *DRED*

Historians do not know why the slave Sam changed his name to Dred. In 1957, Carl Brent Swisher of Johns Hopkins University wrote:

> It is said that during his early years he was labeled not sonorously and in some undefined sense ominously as Dred Scott but by the ordinary name of Sam. We are tempted to wonder, indeed, whether the case name of Sam Scott v. Sandford would have stirred the American people as did the one we know so well. However that may be, what concerns us is that he gave name to a case that embodied all the boiling fury, the frustration, the rage, the indignation and the vibrant idealism that had long been building over the issues of slavery.[2]

slave was Sam, but it is not known why Sam changed his name to Dred Scott. Said to be of pure African descent, Scott was a short, dark-skinned man who could not read or write. But this determined man would be remembered in one of the most important cases to come before the Supreme Court. And even though the Blow family no longer owned him, his relationship with them would help him through his long legal battle for freedom.

## DR. JOHN EMERSON

Emerson studied at the University of Pennsylvania and received his medical degree in 1824. He first served as an army surgeon when he filled in for a sick officer at Jefferson Barracks near Saint Louis in 1832. Emerson later applied for a commission, making military service his life's work. Emerson was approximately 40 years old when he died.

## In Free Territory

In December 1833, Emerson began a career as a surgeon in the US Army at Fort Armstrong in the free state of Illinois. Emerson and Scott would live in the state for more than two years. The area around Fort Armstrong was not well settled and lacked the resources Emerson had enjoyed in the well-developed city of Saint Louis. Emerson requested to be transferred back to Saint Louis more than once, listing diseases and arguments with fellow officers as the reasons. Finally, in May 1836, Emerson received a transfer north to Fort Snelling, near present-day Saint Paul, Minnesota. At the time, the area was part of the Wisconsin Territory—land in which slavery was prohibited by the Missouri Compromise. Additionally, the laws of the newly formed Wisconsin Territory granted settlers in the area the rights of the Northwest Ordinance of 1787, which stated, "There shall be neither slavery nor involuntary servitude in the said Territory, otherwise than in the punishment of crimes, whereof the party shall have been duly convicted."[3] But Scott came along as a slave even though it was forbidden. Historians speculate that as an illiterate man living in a remote area, Scott likely did not know of his legal right to freedom. During the 1820s and 1830s, there were approximately 15 to 20 slaves at Fort Snelling at any given time.[4]

During the time Scott lived at Fort Snelling, he married another slave, Harriet Robinson. Approximately half Scott's age, Harriet was the property of Major Lawrence Taliaferro. Taliaferro performed the marriage ceremony and either gave or sold Harriet to Emerson as a slave. The Scotts would live as husband and wife for more than 20 years. Because they were slaves, however, the marriage had no legal standing.

In October 1837, Emerson was transferred back to Saint Louis, but Scott and Harriet did not accompany him south. Instead, they remained at Fort Snelling as hired-out slaves. The wages they earned for their work were sent back to Emerson. In November, Emerson received orders that he was to be stationed at Fort Jesup in Louisiana. Emerson did not like his new home in

Louisiana, and he requested to be sent back to Fort Snelling. But in the meantime, Emerson married Eliza Irene Sanford, called Irene, on February 6, 1838. Emerson and his new wife sent for Scott and Harriet, who traveled from Fort Snelling to Louisiana in the spring of that year.

Now together with his wife and slaves at Fort Jesup, Emerson again petitioned for a transfer. In one of his letters he wrote, "Even one of my negroes in Saint Louis has sued me for his freedom."[5] Although records of this suit have not been found, this slave could have been Scott attempting to obtain his freedom legally. At the time, Louisiana courts usually ruled in favor of freeing slaves who had lived in free territories. If Scott and Harriet had begun a suit for freedom, it is likely the courts would have ruled in their favor.

Emerson did receive another transfer. That fall, Emerson, his wife, and the Scotts traveled back up the Mississippi River to Fort Snelling, again bringing the two slaves into free territory. According to Reverend Alfred Brunson, a missionary traveling with them, Scott and Harriet gave birth to a baby girl named Eliza on the boat ride back to Fort Snelling. Eliza was born north of the Missouri border in free territory. The Emersons and their

Fort Snelling ca. 1850

slaves arrived at Fort Snelling in October 1838, but they would not stay long. The group traveled south again to Saint Louis in May 1840. Irene Emerson and the Scotts remained in the city while Emerson took a post in Florida. The location did not suit him, and he requested a transfer yet again. But this time, instead of receiving a transfer, Emerson received an honorable discharge from the army.

## Claiming Freedom

Now a civilian, Emerson and his wife, but not the Scotts, moved to Davenport in Iowa Territory in the spring of 1843. Emerson owned land there and built a home for his family. Emerson and his wife welcomed a baby girl in the fall of 1843, but Emerson's health began to fail. He died in December. In his will, Emerson left his estate to his wife, who hired out Scott and Harriet for the next three years. During this time, Scott traveled as a hired slave, possibly to Texas. He returned to Saint Louis in early 1846.

At that time, Scott attempted to buy freedom for himself and his family, but Irene Emerson refused. Soon, Harriet gave birth to another daughter, Lizzie. A Missouri law specifically allowed persons wrongly held in slavery to sue for their freedom. In April 1846, Scott

began his legal suit
for freedom on
behalf of himself,
his wife, and their
two daughters. Scott
could not have
known the massive
impact this action
would take, or how
many years it would
take to reach a
resolution. ∼

> "The declaration shall be in the common form of a declaration for false imprisonment, and shall contain an averment, that the plaintiff, before and at the time of the committing of the grievances, was, and still is, a free person, and that the defendant held, and still holds, him in slavery."[6]
>
> —*MISSOURI STATE STATUTE ALLOWING SLAVES TO SUE FOR THEIR FREEDOM*

# Chapter 6

# Scott v. Emerson

On April 6, 1846, both Dred and Harriet Scott filed petitions with the Saint Louis County Circuit Court. The petitions asked permission to bring suit against Irene Emerson on the basis of their claims to freedom. Their petitions were granted by Judge John Krum, and a **summons** was delivered to Emerson on April 7.

The basis of Scott's suit, known as *Scott v. Emerson*, was that Emerson was holding the Scotts in illegal slavery and had physically beaten them. Scott believed that because he had lived in free territories, he should be a free man. Scott asked for ten dollars in damages. Harriet filed a suit that mirrored her husband's, and at the beginning of the case, the two

## SCOTT'S SPONSORS

Because he was enslaved, Scott did not have money to pay for legal counsel. Throughout his trials, Scott received help from the Blow family, particularly Taylor Blow, the third son of Peter and Elizabeth Blow, Scott's original owners. Scott and the Blow brothers had grown up together. Taylor Blow provided financial support by helping to pay bond for court costs. His brothers, Peter and Henry Taylor Blow, also supported Scott.

suits moved together. The Scotts' daughters' freedom would also be determined in the case. In the suit, it would be important for Scott's attorneys to prove his claim to freedom. If Scott was a slave, then the claims that Emerson had held Scott against his will and beaten him would mean nothing, for that would be an acceptable practice. On November 19, 1846, Emerson filed a plea of not guilty for the charges brought against her.

Throughout June, witnesses were summoned. The trial occurred on June 30, 1847, before Judge Alexander Hamilton. Lawyers from the firm of Alexander Field and David Hall represented Scott, and George W. Goode

**summons**—A notice to appear in court.

Images of Scott, his wife, and his children, *top*, were printed in an illustrated newspaper.

represented Emerson. Samuel Mansfield Bay, the attorney who likely spoke in court on behalf of Scott, had to prove two things. First, he had to prove Scott had been taken to live on free soil. Witnesses testified Scott had indeed lived on free soil in Illinois and at Fort Snelling. Second, Bay had to prove Emerson was now holding Scott as a slave. This point proved difficult to establish, for although witness Samuel Russell had hired the Scotts from Emerson, the **cross-examination** revealed Russell's wife had done the actual hiring and Russell had only supplied the money. Therefore, Russell's **testimony** did not convince the jury Emerson was presently holding the Scotts in slavery, and the decision was made in her favor the same day. Bay immediately moved for a retrial in order to prove Emerson did actually own Scott, and Judge Hamilton granted it. Emerson's lawyers appealed to the Missouri Supreme Court to decide whether the retrial should be held. The state supreme court decided in June 1848 that the new trial could be held.

**cross-examination**—The second questioning of a witness, meant to check or discredit the witness's original testimony.

**testimony**—Something declared in court under oath.

On July 1, 1847, Harriet and Dred Scott each began a new suit, this time against Alexander Sanford (Irene Emerson's father), Samuel Russell, and Irene Emerson. By naming all three people in the suit, there would be no question the Scotts were being held in slavery, and the technicality that decided the first case would not apply. However, on July 31, Judge Hamilton ordered the Scotts to choose one pair of suits—the new suits against the three defendants, or the original suits against Emerson. The Scotts chose to pursue the original suits, which would move to retrial.

While waiting for retrial, the Scotts experienced changes in their personal lives that would affect the cases. Emerson's father died in 1848, and Emerson moved to Massachusetts to live with one of her sisters. Emerson's brother, John Sanford, would take over for Emerson in the case. Up until this point, the Scotts had been working for Russell as Emerson's hired-out slaves. But on March 17, 1848, Judge Hamilton approved Emerson's request to put the Scotts into the sheriff's keeping. The sheriff became responsible for hiring out the Scotts, and he put their wages aside until the court cases were settled. Therefore, while Emerson still maintained her legal claim to the Scotts and any money they earned, she was free from any responsibility to take care of them.

## The Retrial

After many delays, including a major fire and an outbreak of cholera that ravaged the city, the retrial at the Saint Louis circuit court began on January 12, 1850. During the year and a half between the first trial and the second trial, a court date had been set twice and then

### THE MISSOURI JUDGES

Even though previous Missouri Supreme Court decisions had been favorable to slaves, the political situation in Missouri in 1850 was tense. Missouri was geographically vulnerable as a slave state because three of the states bordering it were free.

When *Scott v. Emerson* first came before the court, the three justices were William B. Napton, John F. Ryland, and James H. Birch. Napton and Birch saw this as a chance to make a political move on behalf of the proslavery side. Ryland, knowing their intentions, planned to dissent from their opinion but later changed his mind. Napton delayed writing the opinion, and during his delay, a state election occurred in which Napton and Birch lost their seats. The new justices were William Scott and Hamilton R. Gamble. Justice Gamble was the dissenter when the case was finally settled.

delayed. Emerson had new lawyers, Hugh A. Garland and Lyman D. Norris. Scott's attorney Bay died in the cholera outbreak, and Field and Hall took over the case directly. When the trial date came, Scott's **counsel** made many of the same arguments, but this time the defense had the testimony of Mrs. Russell. Her testimony confirmed she had hired the Scotts from Emerson, and Scott's counsel argued that for Emerson to hire out her slaves proved she was assuming ownership of them. This was the piece of information that had failed to win Scott's freedom in the first trial.

Although Scott's counsel used similar arguments in the new trial, the defense used a few new strategies in defending Emerson. Emerson's lawyers argued that even if Scott had a claim to freedom while he was in free territories, returning to Missouri, a slave state, waived any right to freedom he might have had. This argument supported the belief that, upon Scott's return to slave territory, the laws of that territory prevailed. Additionally, the Emerson counsel argued that when John Emerson brought the Scotts to free territory, he was doing so under the direction of military orders.

**counsel**—A lawyer.

Therefore, the antislavery laws of the territory did not apply because he was instead under military jurisdiction.

However, the legal precedent of *Rachel v. Walker*, decided in 1836, contradicted this argument. In that case, Rachel had sued for her freedom in the Saint Louis courts. Her owner, a US Army officer, had taken her to territories in which slavery was prohibited. He then sold her to William Walker in Saint Louis, and Rachel sued Walker on the premise that her time living in free territories made her free. The lower court ruled against Rachel, stating that because she was the slave of a military officer who could not choose where he was stationed, she had no claim to freedom. She appealed to the Missouri Supreme Court, which ruled in her favor and freed her in 1836. This case had many similarities

## WINNY V. WHITESIDES

In 1824, the Missouri Supreme Court decided the case of *Winny v. Whitesides*. This case is notable as an example of a court from a slave state honoring the laws of a free state. Slave owner Phebe Whitesides moved from the Carolinas to Illinois, bringing her slaves with her, including Winny. After living there for a few years, they moved to the slave state of Missouri. There, the court ruled that the slaves were to be freed due to their time in free territory.

to the Scotts' cases and served as a strong precedent for the court. In addition to this precedent, the defense argued that while Emerson traveled elsewhere, he had left his slaves at Fort Snelling to be hired out. Therefore, the argument of military jurisdiction did not appropriately apply.

Taking into account this evidence and precedent, the court ruled in favor of the Scotts on January 12, the same day the trial had begun. Scott, Harriet, and their two daughters were declared free. In this ruling, Scott had legally been free since 1833 when Emerson had brought him to Fort Armstrong in Illinois. But Emerson's side would not give up. On the same day, Emerson's lawyers filed a **motion** for a new trial. Included in their reasons for a retrial were their statements that "The verdict was contrary to law" and "The verdict was not supported by the Evidence."[1] Judge Hamilton refused, and the Emerson side appealed to the Missouri Supreme Court. In the meantime, the Scotts signed a stipulation declaring that any decision made in Dred's case would also apply to Harriet in her identical case. Delays and a busy state supreme court **docket** meant the court would not reach a decision until 1852. During these two years, numerous legislative and

political happenings would come to weigh heavily upon
the case. An election would mean two new justices sat on
the court.

## A New Compromise

By 1850, the Missouri Compromise of 1820 was falling
apart. Northerners and Southerners continued to debate
the expansion of slavery as new states entered the Union
and new territories were acquired through war with
Mexico. That year, a series of congressional acts known
as the Compromise of 1850 aimed to settle these issues.
In the compromise, California entered the Union as a
free state and the slave trade was banned in the District
of Columbia. These changes pleased the North. But
in addition to these decisions, the Fugitive Slave Act
passed that year, tightening laws relating to the recapture
of escaped slaves and punishing those who helped
escaped slaves. This act pleased Southerners but upset
Northerners because they perceived it as proslavery.

**docket**—A list of cases to be tried.

**motion**—A formal proposal to a court or judge asking for an order,
ruling, or direction.

Also around this time, a legal decision that would come to bear on the *Scott* case was moving to the US Supreme Court. In 1841, a group of slaves traveled from Kentucky into Ohio for a short time. Upon reaching Ohio, they fled to Canada. In the suit, the slaves' owner, Kentuckian Christopher Graham, sued those who had

## THE FUGITIVE SLAVE ACT OF 1850

The Fugitive Slave Act included in the Compromise of 1850 was much harsher than previous laws. Where once the law had merely allowed slaveholders to pursue escaped blacks, now the law required federal law enforcement agents and ordinary citizens to actively aid the slaveholders. Anyone who helped escaped blacks would be fined or even put in prison. Any black—free or escaped from slavery—could be forcibly taken into slavery without a trial if a white person said he or she was a slave.

The law outraged many in the North. Abolitionists hated it, as did those who saw it as infringing on states' rights. Black communities in the North worked hard to protect their own members as well as former slaves newly arriving from the South. Activity on the Underground Railroad—a network of people who helped blacks escape slavery—increased, as did immigration to Canada. Violence broke out more than once as crowds of people, black and white, broke captured blacks out of jail or physically prevented slave catchers from leaving with their captives. The Fugitive Slave Act is generally cited as a major step on the road to the Civil War.

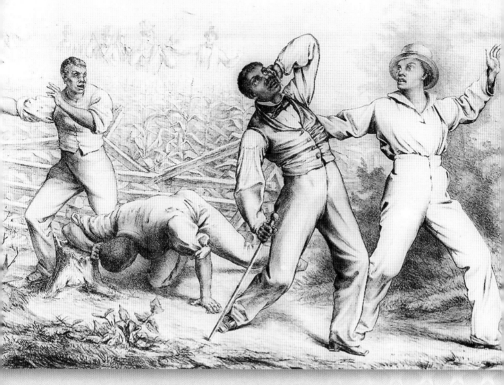

This 1850 illustration condemned the Fugitive Slave Act, showing white masters shooting black slaves.

allegedly helped the slaves escape to Canada, including steamboat owner Jacob Strader. The defense maintained that the slaves, because they had traveled to Ohio, were free men when they escaped to Canada. The court's opinion declared each state had the right to decide whether its inhabitants were free or enslaved. Therefore, the slaves were subject to the laws of Kentucky, the home state, not Ohio. The Supreme Court's 1851 ruling in the case, *Strader v. Graham*, set a strong legal precedent in favor of states' rights and reversion.

# The Decision Reversed

Before the three justices of the state supreme court, Emerson's lawyers took into account these recent events. They referenced *Strader v. Graham* and argued that freedom laws from Illinois could not be applied to slaves now living in Missouri. Hall appealed to the Missouri courts' history of ruling in favor of slaves in cases such as Scott's.

In a vote of two to one, the Missouri Supreme Court reversed the lower court's decision on March 22, 1852, and declared Scott and his family were still slaves. This decision ignored the legal precedents that had been set in previous decades. In his **majority opinion**, Justice William Scott addressed the changing opinions regarding slavery. He acknowledged the previous court decisions Hall referred to, but he believed slave states were not bound to comply with the antislavery laws of other states. His opinion dealt with these conflicting laws. He stated,

> *Times are not now as they were when the former decisions on this subject were made. . . . [The state of Missouri] is willing to assume her full responsibility for the existence of slavery within her limits, nor does she seek to share or divide it with others.*[2]

Justice Hamilton Gamble disagreed with the majority opinion and wrote a **dissent**. Believing slaves were more than property, he disagreed on the basis that the Missouri courts had already decided this issue repeatedly, and that these decisions were made during times of relative peace and did not reflect current trends in thought regarding slavery. Gamble's opinion hinted that his fellow judges had caved to public opinion and used the case as a political attack against the antislavery movement. Although the court had ruled against the Scotts, their suit was not over. Instead, it would take a new form as it moved to a higher court. ~

**dissent**—An official written statement of a Supreme Court justice who disagrees with the majority decision.

**majority opinion**—An explanation of the reasoning behind the majority decision of the Supreme Court.

# Chapter 7

# The Case against Sanford

**A**fter the Missouri Supreme Court ruled against Scott, the case against Emerson was over because Scott did not appeal to the US Supreme Court. However, Scott soon began a new case, and this time, the case was heard in the Missouri district of the US Circuit Court. The case originated in circuit court rather than a lower court because it involved citizens of more than one state. On November 2, 1853, Scott began a suit against John Sanford, Irene Emerson's brother who had taken over her legal affairs in Missouri. The suit of *Dred Scott v. John F. A. Sandford* alleged an action of **trespass vi et armis** had occurred. Scott accused Sanford of

## ROSWELL FIELD TAKES THE CASE

After 1848, the Scotts were under the charge of a Missouri sheriff. Charles Edmund LaBeaume, who was related to the Blow family through marriage, hired them out for five dollars a month. The Blow family was no longer able to pay Scott's legal fees, but LaBeaume was sympathetic to their desire to help the Scotts. LaBeaume was a lawyer, and he asked colleague Roswell Field about the case. After giving his opinion, Field agreed to take the case as Scott's counsel.

assaulting Scott and his family, and he asked for $9,000 in damages.

Scott had another new lawyer, Roswell Field, a Vermont native who stood firmly against slavery. He was not related to Scott's previous lawyer, Alexander Field. He took the case **pro bono**, and there is some evidence suggesting he specifically wished to move the case to the Supreme Court to make it a **test case** on the various issues of slavery and freedom in the territories. Likewise, there is evidence Sanford's supporters also wanted the case to move to the highest court. Supporters of both

**pro bono**—Expecting no payment.
**test case**—A case that is likely to set a precedent for future rulings.
**trespass vi et armis**—Wrongful conduct with force and violence.

parties to the case wanted a definitive ruling from the Supreme Court.

To move the case forward into the federal courts, Field highlighted the differing jurisdictions between the defendant and the plaintiff—Scott was acting as a citizen of Missouri and brought suit against Sanford, a citizen of New York. This was a risky move. If the court accepted the case, it would be an implicit acceptance of Scott as a citizen of Missouri, which would go against the precedent of *Strader v. Graham*. For his part, Sanford challenged the very legitimacy of the suit. He argued that because Scott was a black man of African descent, Scott was not a citizen and had no right to sue.

After some consideration, Judge Robert W. Wells upheld Scott's right to sue in federal court. However, he made explicit that citizenship, in this case, meant that Scott was a resident of Missouri—but Scott was not a full citizen entitled to the rights declared by the Constitution. The "citizenship" granted to Scott gave him the right to sue and

> Because he is a negro of African descent— his ancestors were of pure African blood and were brought into this country and sold as negro slaves."[1]
>
> —SANFORD'S ASSERTION THAT SCOTT WAS NOT A US CITIZEN

be sued in court, but little more. Wells was not making a blanket ruling to declare all blacks citizens, an issue that had been ruled on by state courts but had not been decisively decided at the federal court level.

## The Case at Court

Sanford entered a plea of not guilty. His plea acknowledged he had laid hands on his slaves but in a manner permissible for a slaveholder. The case was heard on May 15, 1854, with Garland continuing to act as counsel for Sanford. It was a quiet trial that did not attract much attention. No witnesses were called. Instead, Field read a statement of facts outlining Scott's travels with Emerson and urged the court to rule in Scott's favor. By this time, the question was no longer whether Scott had lived in a free territory or to whom he belonged as a slave. Rather, a larger issue was at stake: did living in a free territory render a slave free if he or she returned to a slave state?

The ruling came in favor of Sanford, agreeing with the decision of the Missouri court. The circuit court decided that because Scott had sued for freedom while living in Missouri, the laws of that state must be applied, rendering Scott still a slave. If Scott had sued while living in free territory, such as Illinois, he might have been emancipated according to that state's laws. Judge Wells later wrote in a letter that he personally wished the law had been in favor of Scott, for he had taken an interest in the slave. Scott, through Field, immediately appealed to the US Supreme Court.

## Finding New Counsel

As the case moved to Washington DC, Scott needed to find an excellent attorney to argue his case there. With little money to pay for a lawyer, Field and Scott hoped to find an attorney who would work pro bono. Scott made his plea through a 12-page pamphlet highlighting the details of the case. In a portion attributed to Scott, the pamphlet declared,

> I have no money to pay anybody at Washington to speak for me. My fellow-men, can any of you help me in my day of trial? Will nobody speak for me at Washington, even without hope of other reward than the blessings of a poor black man and his family? I do not know. I can only pray that some good heart will be moved by pity to do that for me which I cannot do for myself; and that if the right

*is on my side it may be so declared by the high court to which I have appealed.*[2]

Nobody responded to the plea for help.

On December 24, 1854, Field wrote to Montgomery Blair, a former Saint Louis attorney who had moved to Washington in the early 1850s and had experience arguing before the Supreme Court. Field hoped Blair or another attorney there would take the case. Field knew the attorney who took the case would have to feel passionately about the issue in order to work for free or for little pay. After enlisting the help of abolitionist journalist Gamaliel Bailey, who agreed to pay for court costs, Blair accepted.

In handing off the case to Blair, Field wrote a long letter to the new attorney, outlining not only the history of the case but also the potential political implications.

89

Montgomery Blair agreed to serve as Scott's lawyer.

First, Field addressed the issue of black citizenship. Judge Wells had allowed for Scott to sue in the federal court, giving slaves an incomplete form of state citizenship. This had profound implications, especially in relation to the newly passed Fugitive Slave Act. If Wells's decision were applied universally, slaves could bring their masters to court before a jury. Field assumed this issue would not come up in the Supreme Court ruling, but expressed his interest in garnering an opinion nonetheless.

Field also discussed the issue of reattachment. The US circuit court ruled that once the Scotts had returned to Missouri from free territory, the laws of slavery reattached themselves, rendering the Scotts slaves. This had been a long-argued issue, as the courts had for years wrestled with the idea of state sovereignty and the principle of "once free, always free." The attorneys knew the decision from the Supreme Court would have wide implications.

The Sanford side would also gain considerable experience in its new attorneys, Reverdy Johnson and Henry S. Geyer, both of whom offered their services at no cost to Sanford. Johnson had served as attorney general under President Zachary Taylor and was a successful and well-known constitutional lawyer. Geyer was a Missouri senator with many proslavery clients. The fact both men agreed to take the case at the Supreme Court level was evidence the case would be an important one. ∼

## THE SUPREME COURT

The US Supreme Court is the head of the federal court system and is the only court specifically established by the US Constitution. However, the Constitution did not create the structure of the court system. The first congress passed the Judiciary Act of 1789, which established district courts, circuit courts, and the concepts of a chief justice and associate justices. Through the nineteenth century, each Supreme Court justice also presided over a US circuit court when the Supreme Court was in recess. This practice ended in 1891 when the court of appeals was created.

# Chapter 8

# Before the Supreme Court

*E*ven though the Supreme Court officially received the case on December 30, 1854, the *Scott* case was behind many others and would sit for more than a year. Around this time, the riots of Bleeding Kansas consumed that state and highlighted the need for a judicial decision regarding the right of Congress to regulate slavery in the territories. Also during that time, Blair hoped to find assistance from other attorneys, but nobody stepped forward to work on the *Scott* case with him. He would stand alone in the Supreme Court.

Finally, on Monday, February 11, 1856, the court began to hear the **oral arguments**, which would last four days. The justices, led by Chief Justice Taney, entered quietly in their black gowns. Besides Taney, the other eight justices were John A. Campbell, John Catron, Benjamin R. Curtis, Peter V. Daniel, Robert C. Grier, John McLean, Samuel Nelson, and James M. Wayne. Of the nine justices, Taney, Campbell, Catron, Daniel, and Wayne generally supported slavery.

## First Arguments

Oral arguments before the Supreme Court at that time were not recorded word for word. Therefore, the arguments of the *Scott* case were preserved in the written **briefs** submitted by both sides prior to the hearing and in fragments in newspaper articles. Blair's first argument addressed the citizenship issue, which Judge Wells had upheld by allowing Scott to sue in the federal court, even if it was only a limited citizenship. Drawing upon a previous legal decision from the Kentucky Supreme Court, *Amy v. Smith*, Blair argued that the right to vote did not necessarily determine citizenship, but instead argued, "It appears . . . that the essence of citizenship is

**brief**—A document that establishes the legal argument of a case.
**oral argument**—A spoken presentation of a legal case by a lawyer.

Until the Supreme Court Building was completed in 1935, the Supreme Court met in this chamber in the US Capitol to decide cases.

the right of protection of life and liberty, to acquire and enjoy property and equal taxation."[1] Blair called Scott a *"quasi* citizen."[2] Thus, Blair spent a good amount of time arguing for a confirmation of the lower court's decision regarding black citizenship, at least for the right to sue in federal court. Without the establishment of this point, the case could be thrown out.

Blair then argued for Scott's freedom. His case rested on the Missouri Compromise Act, which stated,

> . . . in all that territory ceded by France to the United States, . . . which lies north of thirty-six degrees and thirty minutes north latitude, not included within the limits of the state, contemplated by this act, slavery and involuntary servitude, otherwise than in the punishment of crimes, whereof the parties

## ELIZA SCOTT

During his initial arguments, Blair made a special case for the freedom of Eliza Scott. Eliza was born on a boat in the Mississippi River traveling north in 1838. Technically, she was born north of the Missouri border, in Illinois Territory. Blair argued that, according to the Missouri Compromise and the Illinois Constitution, Eliza's place of birth should make her free.

*shall have been duly convicted, shall be, and is hereby, forever prohibited.*[3]

Blair argued that Scott's claim to freedom was legitimate because Scott had traveled north of this determined border and lived there for an extended period of time. But this argument assumed Congress had the power to prohibit slavery in the territories. Blair argued Congress did have that power and the framers of the Constitution had intended to stop the spread of slavery.

## GAINING INTEREST

Journalists reported on the case with increasing frequency as the arguments were made and during the following break. In February, journalist James Harvey of the *New York Tribune* predicted the court would rule against Scott and would avoid a decision on the question of congressional power over slavery in the territories. In April, Harvey reported that the court was divided on whether to rule on black citizenship.

But after that, the case was buried under news about the upcoming presidential election. James Buchanan would beat out John C. Frémont and Millard Fillmore. The issue of slavery in the territories was a dividing issue in the race, and by the time it was over, the nation was looking to the Supreme Court for a final ruling on the issue.

Next, Geyer and Johnson spoke on behalf of Sanford. They argued that Scott, a black slave, was not a citizen of Missouri and did not have the right to sue in federal court. Scott's right to sue had been upheld in the lower court by Judge Wells. But at this point, Sanford's lawyers attacked the case from a new angle by questioning the legitimacy of the Missouri Compromise.

After the arguments were made, the justices discussed the case from February until May. But they were split on what their ruling should cover. Taney, Curtis, Wayne, and Daniel were in favor of discussing and ruling on black citizenship, but McLean, Catron, Grier, and Campbell opposed ruling on the issue. Nelson was undecided. The justices also argued whether the court even had jurisdiction in the case. Because the court was so closely split, the justices determined a reargument was needed to determine whether the issue of black citizenship should be decided at all. The reargument would take place in the next term, after the presidential election.

## Reargument

On December 15, the reargument began. This time, Blair was not alone. George T. Curtis, brother of Justice Benjamin R. Curtis, agreed to help, specifically in establishing the **constitutionality** of the Missouri Compromise.

First, Blair spoke about the citizenship issue, highlighting differences between the civil rights of citizens, such as using the courts, and the political privileges of citizens, such as voting. Blair also addressed instances in which federal laws had used the term *citizen* to mean "inhabitant," using this argument to prove Scott, as an inhabitant of Missouri, enjoyed the civil right to sue in court.

In response, Geyer argued that in order to obtain federal citizenship, a person must first be a citizen of the state. Born into slavery and never **naturalized**, Scott was not a US citizen, even if traveling to a free region had made him a quasi-citizen of a free state or territory. Therefore, Geyer argued that the lower court, under Judge Wells, had been wrong to allow Scott to sue in federal court. However, Geyer continued his arguments in case the Supreme Court did side with Judge Wells. In addressing the issue of freedom, Geyer asserted that

**constitutionality**—Being in accordance with a constitution.
**naturalized**—Became a US citizen.

Scott's time in Illinois and at Fort Snelling were travels mandated by the US military. Furthermore, in returning to Missouri, the slavery laws of that state returned to Scott.

Blair refuted the first argument by claiming that Emerson did in fact make these military posts his home, appealing to the important distinction between traveling through free territory and living in free territory. As to the second argument, the issue of reattachment, Blair pointed out that the Missouri court's decision had been in direct opposition to the precedents of that state and demonstrated giving in to political pressure about slavery.

## Congress and the Constitution

However, at this point in the case, the congressional right to legislate slavery in the territories became crucial. Geyer and Johnson argued that even during his time in free territory, Scott was never freed because Congress did not have the authority to ban slavery in the territories. The argument rested on the interpretation of Article IV, Section 3 of the Constitution, which states:

> *The Congress shall have Power to dispose of and make all needful Rules and Regulations respecting*

*the Territory or other Property belonging to the United States; and nothing in this Constitution shall be so construed as to Prejudice any Claims of the United States, or of any particular State.*[4]

Geyer and Johnson argued that this article only provided Congress with the power to make basic laws

## THE CHIEF JUSTICE

Roger Brooke Taney was born in 1777 in Maryland. He belonged to a wealthy slaveholding family. Taney attended Dickinson College and had his own law practice before beginning his political career in the Maryland State Senate. He became the state attorney general in 1827 and the US attorney general in 1831 under President Andrew Jackson. When Jackson initially nominated Taney to the Supreme Court in 1835, the Senate blocked the nomination. But by 1836, the Senate makeup had changed to favor the nomination and Taney became the chief justice that year. He was 59 years old, and few believed he would remain chief justice for long. However, he would sit on the bench for almost 30 years.

Taney favored states' rights and a strong judicial branch. He was not passionately proslavery, and he had emancipated his own slaves in 1818. However, Taney was committed to the preservation of Southern values. In Southern culture, owning slaves heightened a person's standing in society. Any attack on slavery was an attack on the Southern notions of honor and respect.

necessary for the temporary governing of a territory, and that this power arose only because a territory did not fall under a state's jurisdiction. In their view, congressional power to prohibit slavery in the territories was not explicitly given in the Constitution. Blair and Curtis interpreted it in the opposite manner: that this power was implicitly given.

## The Majority Decision

On March 6, 1857, Taney and the other justices entered the courtroom to deliver their opinions. By a ruling of 7–2, Scott was still a slave. But the opinion would also include rulings on the constitutionality of the Missouri Compromise and the citizenship of blacks, and the justices were far from in agreement. Nevertheless, Taney's opinion was recorded as the majority opinion of the court, even though not every justice agreed with him on every point.

Taney's opinion was layered. First, he had to deliver the court's opinion on the jurisdictional issue. Did Scott have the right to sue in federal court? Was the case standing before the Supreme Court legitimate? If the answer was no, then the case must be thrown out.

In discussing citizens of the United States and whether blacks were included in that group, Taney wrote,

> *The question before us is, whether the class of persons described in the plea in abatement [blacks] compose a portion of this people, and are constituent members of this sovereignty? We think they are not, and that they are not included, and were not intended to be included, under the word "citizens" in the Constitution, and can therefore claim none of the rights and privileges which that instrument provides for and secures to citizens of the United States.*[5]

Taney's decision stated that the Declaration of Independence, which proclaims all men are created equal, clearly excluded blacks, and that the Constitution designated blacks as a separate class incapable of citizenship. Taney's decision went against the ruling of Judge Wells, and Taney declared the suit should have been thrown out by the lower court for this reason. But despite this, Taney did not stop there. Even though his decision made it plain the case was illegitimate, he took the opportunity to rule on the other controversial issues at hand—issues for which the public was clamoring for a definitive opinion.

Taney's opinion declared Scott was not free because the Missouri Compromise was unconstitutional. Congress or any other body did not have the constitutional power to prohibit slavery in the territories. In regards to the territorial clause in the Constitution, Taney discussed the context in which the Constitution was written. Stating that the clause was a "special provision" written in a state

## TANEY DELAYS PUBLICATION

After the majority opinion was announced, the public was anxious for the individual opinions of each justice to be published. Taney's opinion had been published in part by a news reporter who had witnessed its reading, but Taney delayed publishing his official opinion. The public—and dissenter Justice Curtis—wondered why, for the rules of the court required opinions be submitted immediately. Curtis wrote to Taney to request a copy, but Taney refused to give him one, accusing Curtis of wanting to use it for political purposes. By the end of April, Taney's opinion had still not been submitted and published.

The *Scott* decision was officially published in May. After reading it, Curtis claimed Taney's opinion had been heavily altered, with new material added in direct rebuttal to Curtis's opinion. Although Taney denied these allegations, historical records show the official published opinion was as much as 50 percent longer than the opinion read in court, implying Taney did alter his opinion after the fact to offer arguments against Curtis.

of "emergency, and nothing more," Taney argued that the clause could not be applied to the *Scott* case because the territory Scott lived in had not been the territory originally discussed in the Constitution.[6]

Taney then discussed the nature of property and its protection by the Constitution. In relation to slaves as property, he argued traveling into free territory did not free a slave, writing,

> It is the opinion of the court that the act of Congress which prohibited a citizen from holding and owning property of this kind in the territory of the United States north of the line therein mentioned, is not warranted by the Constitution, and is therefore void; and that neither Dred Scott himself, nor any of his family, were made free by being carried into this territory; even if they had been carried there by the owner, with the intention of becoming a permanent resident.[7]

Taney based his argument on the Fifth Amendment, which guarantees citizens will not be deprived of life or property without **due process of law**. Taney believed

---

**due process of law**—A basic principle in the US legal system that requires fairness in the government's dealings with people.

Chief Justice Taney did not believe blacks should have the same rights as whites.

freeing a slave owner's slaves because the owner had taken them into a US territory would be depriving the owner of property without due process. Finally, Taney referenced the precedent of *Strader v. Graham* and stated that once Scott returned to Missouri from Illinois, Missouri law overtook any law of Illinois that might have applied in that state. The final ruling was that the case must return to the lower court and be thrown out, because Scott did not have the right to sue in federal court. Justices Wayne, Nelson, Grier, Daniel, Campbell, and Catron wrote concurring opinions, although not every justice agreed on every point made by Taney in his majority opinion.

## The Dissents

Only two justices dissented from the majority opinion: McLean and Curtis. McLean, the strongest antislavery justice on the court, opposed the decision that Scott could not sue. McLean stated,

> *Being born under our Constitution and laws, no naturalization is required, as one of foreign birth, to make him a citizen. The most general and appropriate definition of the term citizen is 'a freeman.' Being a freeman, and having his domicile in a State different from that of the defendant, he is a citizen within the act of Congress, and the courts of the Union are open to him.*[8]

McLean defended slavery as a state institution, declaring each state's constitution to be respected. In McLean's view, Scott was emancipated by living for two years in Illinois and two more at Fort Snelling, and

## CURTIS AND THE INTERPRETATION OF LAWS

In his dissent, Justice Curtis warned about the dangers of allowing political opinions to enter into judicial decisions. He wrote:

> When a strict interpretation of the Constitution, according to the fixed rules which govern the interpretation of laws, is abandoned, and the theoretical opinions of individuals are allowed to control its meaning, we have no longer a Constitution; we are under the government of individual men, who for the time being have power to declare what the Constitution is, according to their own views of what it ought to mean.[9]

this freedom was not to be reversed by his being taken unwillingly back to Missouri.

Justice Curtis wrote the longest opinion of all—16 pages longer than the majority opinion. Curtis himself was not antislavery, but his opinion defended states' rights. Curtis spent a few paragraphs establishing that at the time the Constitution was written, numerous states had allowed blacks the right to vote, which implied their citizenship. He also tied citizenship to birth. He said,

> *I can find nothing in the Constitution which, . . . deprives of their citizenship any class of persons who were citizens of the United States at the time of its*

*adoption, or who should be native-born citizens of any State after its adoption; nor any power enabling Congress to disfranchise persons born on the soil of any State, and entitled to citizenship of such State by its Constitution and laws.*[10]

Curtis also included a lengthy argument for the constitutionality of the Missouri Compromise and the Northwest Ordinance. He noted that in Congress, the Northwest Ordinance had been signed by 14 men who had been part of the Constitutional Convention and also by President Washington. Curtis used this as evidence that these men, who framed the Constitution, were making a statement for the constitutional right for Congress to limit slavery in the territories.

Clearly, the court was divided on almost every facet of the far-reaching decision. And the many reactions from the US public would mirror the many opinions of the nine men who had heard the case in the highest tribunal. ~

Justice Curtis faced several bitter Supreme Court battles and resigned after only six years on the bench.

# Chapter 9

# The Conclusions Reached

With the court ruling the case should have been dismissed because Scott lacked the legal right to sue, the matter could have ended there. But Taney's decision had said so much more. Because Taney was determined to take on the issues of slavery in the territories and of black citizenship, his decision affected more people than just Sanford, Scott, and Scott's family. The court's majority opinion was clearly political. Perhaps Taney intended to settle the issue through the Supreme Court once and for all, thus quieting any congressional debate on the subject. But his plan backfired. Instead of quieting the nation, the ruling sent the country into an uproar.

The implications of the black citizenship decision were far reaching. Until that point, individual state courts had ruled in cases regarding black citizenship, but their rulings fell under Article IV, Section 2 of the Constitution, which discusses privileges given to state citizens. At the time of the *Scott* trial, the courts had not made a definitive decision on the US citizenship of blacks, so the Taney decision that blacks were not US citizens had been long awaited and carried tremendous weight.

The decision was devastating to blacks. The decision said blacks were noncitizens who could claim none of the rights or protections the Constitution gives to citizens. It gave constitutional, federal justification for racism. States did not have to give rights to any free blacks.

> " To be black in America in the late 1850s was to live in a land that said you didn't have a future."[1]
>
> —*DAVID W. BLIGHT, PROFESSOR OF HISTORY AND BLACK STUDIES, AMHERST COLLEGE*

The decision regarding the Missouri Compromise was an especially heavy blow to the newly formed Republican Party, which stood against the expansion of slavery in the territories. The Supreme Court's ruling against the Missouri Compromise threatened to destroy the party's entire platform. The majority opinion in the *Scott* case declared slavery was solely in the hands of the states, and in the territories, any ban on slavery was unconstitutional, federal or otherwise. Congress had been prohibiting slavery in the territories since the Northwest Ordinance passed 70 years earlier. The ruling overturned this long practice.

## The Public Responds

The Republican Party responded angrily to the ruling in the *Scott* case because it feared this would pave the way for the nationalization of slavery. The decision implied even free states could be open to slavery, for slaveholders living in a free state could keep their slaves for an indefinite amount of time. Many, including Abraham Lincoln, saw the decision as a threat to democracy.

Newspapers gave thorough coverage of the decision. The *New York Tribune*, whose founder and editor, Horace Greeley, was an outspoken antislavery advocate, published many articles on the subject. On March 7, a *Tribune* editorial reviewed the decision and attacked the court, stating, "This decision, we need hardly say, is entitled to just so much moral weight as would be the judgment of a majority of those congregated in any Washington bar-room."[2] On March 19, the *New York Independent* quoted a portion of Taney's decision and called it a "horrible hand-book of tyranny."[3] And an article in another New York paper, the *Daily Times*, demonstrated a belief that the radical decision would only strengthen the abolitionist cause.

In response, many Southern newspapers defended the court's decision, fueling an editorial war of words. The strongest editorial war was waged between the *New York Tribune* and the *Union*, from Washington DC, which followed the view of the Buchanan administration and the Democratic Party. On March 12, 1857, a

*Union* editorial supporting the decision declared the Supreme Court:

> is elevated above the schemes of party politics, and shielded alike from the effects of sudden passion and of popular prejudice. Little motive, therefore, can the venerable jurists who compose that tribunal have for a deviation from the true principles of law.[4]

Democratic writers in this and other papers condemned those who opposed the ruling as rebels against the United States and celebrated the victory the court had given their cause, submitting to the ruling as the decisive law of the land and calling for others to do the same.

In general, most white Southerners approved of the ruling, for although they disagreed on how slavery should be governed and protected, the decision supported their overall position on slavery. The decision also received some support in the North, especially among Democrats. Many of these supporters were hopeful the decision would put an end to the slavery conflict, or they approved of the decisions for racist reasons.

In 1850, Irene Emerson moved to Springfield, Massachusetts, and remarried. Her new husband, Dr. Calvin C. Chaffee, was a Massachusetts congressman of strong abolitionist convictions with connections to the Republican Party. After the case became public, Chaffee's connection to the case was revealed. As newspapers criticized his hypocrisy, an embarrassed Chaffee denied having any knowledge of the suit until after it was noticed for trial.

In addition to appearing in the newspapers, opinions about the *Scott* decision were also heard from the pulpit. Blair reported hearing McLean's decision read aloud at church. George B. Cheever, a New York pastor, delivered a series of powerful antislavery sermons, equating slavery with evil and encouraging people to disobey the Supreme Court's ruling because it was an affront to God.

## Political Criticism

After the justices' official reports were published in May, legal experts began to publicly analyze the decision, often in calmer language than the editorials used. A few spoke up in favor of the decision, but the majority of these experts criticized the court. The questions these professionals brought up would continue to be discussed for decades after the case was decided. Many doubted Taney's majority opinion truly represented the majority of the justices, as evidenced by the lengthy individual opinions most wrote to explain their views.

Others raised the question of **dictum**. A dictum ruling is not necessary to determine the outcome of the case, and therefore it is not legally binding. This argument was based on Taney's primary decision: if blacks could not sue in court and therefore, the case should be thrown out and the rulings should stop there. Thus, many questioned the legitimacy of the court's further rulings, especially on the constitutionality of the Missouri Compromise. On this topic, Justice Curtis wrote in his dissent: " . . . I feel obliged to say that, in my opinion, such an exertion of judicial power transcends the limits of the authority of the court. . . ."[5] Republicans agreed, and after the decision, they maintained Congress did have the right to prohibit slavery in the territories. One Boston lawyer, Timothy

dictum—A judge's expressed opinion on a point other than the exact issue involved in deciding a case.

Farrar, referred to the court's decisions past the issue of jurisdiction as "usurpation."[6]

In addition to criticism from lawyers and the legal community, Taney's decision faced rebellion from the state legislatures. The legislatures of Connecticut and Maine soon passed antislavery legislation opposing the *Scott* decision. Other states, including New Hampshire, New York, Pennsylvania, and Ohio, quickly moved to pass similar measures, but not all would be successful. At the time, people who spoke out about black rights were ridiculed for their views on racial equality. For example, a

## DEFENDING THE COURT

In the summer of 1857, after the official opinions of the court were published, a New York journalist commented on the number of state legislatures that had rushed to pass laws condemning the Supreme Court decision. The writer noted:

*Very serious damage to the reputation of the nation, as well as to the cause of good order, was done by these hasty proceedings. . . . The confidence of the people in the honesty of that branch of the Government . . . has been seriously shaken. . . . In the bitterness of our dissent, therefore, . . . we must be very careful not to stigmatize the Supreme Court as an enemy to freedom. . . .[7]*

An advertisement for published copies of Taney's defense of his decision proposed amendment to the New York Constitution that would allow blacks the right to vote was struck down after newspapers condemned those who supported it.

Even members of the Supreme Court defied the decision. In May 1857, in a case in his circuit district involving a black **litigant**, Justice McLean did not apply the *Scott* decision and allowed a black to sue.

In light of this criticism and the judicial defiance, Taney felt compelled to write a paper in his own defense. In the paper, published in September 1858, Taney discussed the racial attitudes of generations past, namely the British monarchy and the views of the Founding Fathers at the time of the Constitutional Convention, which he had referred to in his original opinion. In his supplement, he referred to the distinctive lines drawn between white and black people as "indelible."[8] Publishing this opinion is evidence of the strong conviction Taney felt about the decisions he had made. But despite his passionate feelings, his decisions would not have the longevity he hoped. ~

**litigant**—A person bringing a lawsuit to court.

# Chapter 10

# Amending the Constitution

*S*cott had lost his case, but he had not lost his cause. In May 1857, Calvin Chaffee, Emerson's husband, transferred ownership of the Scott family to Taylor Blow. Blow formally emancipated the family on May 26. After an 11-year legal battle for freedom in the courts, Scott was manumitted by the son of his original owner. As a free man, Scott continued to live in Saint Louis with his family, where he worked at a hotel. But Scott would not enjoy his freedom for long. Sick with tuberculosis, a disease of the lungs, Scott died on September 17, 1858, and was buried in the Saint Louis Wesleyan Cemetery. On September 21, a *New York Times* journalist noted, "It is not well to let the great pass away without note and worthy honor. Dred Scott is dead. . . . few men who have achieved greatness have won it so effectually as this black champion."[1] But Scott's death certainly did not mean the death of the issues brought up by the case that bore his name.

## Lincoln, Douglas, and Dred Scott

Politically, the *Scott* decision would have lasting effects, particularly on the Democratic Party. In 1858, Abraham Lincoln ran against the incumbent Stephen Douglas in the race for one of Illinois's US Senate seats, and slavery once again proved a central issue. On June 16, at the Illinois Republican Convention, Lincoln delivered his "house divided" speech. In this speech, Lincoln expressed his opinion that a conspiracy between Douglas, Taney, Buchanan, and former president Franklin Pierce had been put in place to nationalize slavery, with the *Scott* decision being one

> " I believe this government cannot endure, permanently, half slave and half free. I do not expect the Union to be dissolved; I do not expect the house to fall; but I do expect it will cease to be divided. It will become all one thing, or all the other."[2]
>
> —ABRAHAM LINCOLN, JUNE 16, 1858, "HOUSE DIVIDED" SPEECH

Lincoln's debates with Douglas helped raise his profile and contributed to his 1860 presidential win.

of the key components. He would say much more on the topic of slavery, as he and Douglas engaged in a series of debates leading up to the election.

At the time, Douglas was drawing apart from the Democratic Party. In 1857, Douglas had spoken out against a proslavery Kansas Constitution. Passed in Lecompton, the drafting of that constitution had been full of controversy and fraud, and Douglas, a longtime supporter of popular sovereignty, rejected it because he did not believe it was a true representation of the will of the people. This stance put him at odds with President Buchanan and much of the Democratic Party, which labeled him a traitor for speaking out against the proslavery document. Many Republicans praised Douglas for his stance against the fraudulent Kansas Constitution.

Therefore, during the Lincoln-Douglas debates, Lincoln sought to strike down any Republican sympathy Douglas might have earned. Lincoln again grouped Douglas with the proslavery conspirators who sought to nationalize slavery. In return, Douglas criticized Lincoln's defense of black rights.

The *Scott* decision would prove to be one of the most polarizing topics brought up in the debates. Douglas defended the decision. In response, Lincoln argued that Douglas's idea of popular sovereignty—that is, the states should make their own decisions about slavery—could not coexist with the Supreme Court opinion, which stated that the territories could not prohibit slavery. When questioned about the supposed inconsistency of his beliefs, Douglas responded that citizens in new territories could choose to prohibit slavery through the laws they passed. This statement directly contradicted the *Scott* decision and angered many proslavery Southerners, contributing to a great split in the Democratic Party.

## Civil War

Douglas managed to gain Senate reelection in 1858, but Lincoln went on to win the presidential election

## THE COURT DISSOLVES

When the Civil War began, the members of the Supreme Court had changed since the 1857 *Scott* decision was issued. In 1861, Chief Justice Taney still sat on the bench, but Curtis had resigned in 1858 after quarrelling with him about the publication of their respective opinions. Justice Daniel had died in 1860 and McLean died the following year. After the Civil War broke out, Justice Campbell resigned to join the Confederacy.

of 1860. Southern states were outraged, and on December 20, 1860, South Carolina seceded from the Union, with Mississippi, Florida, Alabama, Georgia, Louisiana, and Texas following soon after. In total, 11 states would secede. In February 1861, Jefferson Davis was elected president of the newly formed Confederate States of America. This provisional government's constitution explicitly protected the right to own slaves.

Lincoln was inaugurated on March 4, 1861, and Taney administered the oath of office. Determined to protect the Union, Lincoln refused to accept secession in his inaugural address. In April, the first shots of the Civil War were fired at Fort Sumter in South Carolina. The war would claim more American lives than any other in US history. It would also have a profound effect on decisions made in the *Scott* case.

## The Road to Emancipation

With the war underway and many Southern Congress members absent, the remaining members passed several laws and acts relating to slaves. In April 1862, Congress offered financial aid to states that agreed to gradual emancipation. That same month, Congress abolished slavery in the District of Columbia. In June, Congress passed and Lincoln signed laws that prohibited slavery in the territories. Though this action directly defied the *Scott* decision, the *Scott* case was not mentioned during congressional debate or in news reports.

In September 1862, a few days after the Union victory at Antietam, President Lincoln issued a warning: if the states of the Confederacy did not return to the Union by January 1, 1863, all slaves in these states would be declared free. The states of the Confederacy did not comply. On January 1, Lincoln issued his Emancipation Proclamation, declaring these slaves free and allowing slaves to enlist to fight for the Union. Although the proclamation did not free all the slaves immediately, allowing slaves to enlist on behalf of the

## THE REELECTION OF LINCOLN

In 1864, in the midst of the Civil War, the possibility of reelection did not look good for Lincoln. In the presidential race, he faced Democrat George B. McClellan. But late in the summer, a few key Union victories were enough to encourage voters to reelect Lincoln to the White House for a second term. Lincoln took the oath of office on March 4, 1865, and the Civil War ended the following month. On April 14, Lincoln was shot in the head by actor and Confederate sympathizer John Wilkes Booth. Lincoln died the next morning.

The Emancipation Proclamation earned Lincoln the nickname the Great Emancipator.

Union was a great help to the North. On April 9, 1865, Confederate General Robert E. Lee surrendered to Union General Ulysses S. Grant at Appomattox Court House in Virginia. After four long years, the Civil War was over.

## Slavery Abolished

The Civil War was fought to preserve the Union. However, one tremendously important outcome of the war was the abolition of slavery. On December 6, 1865, the Thirteenth Amendment to the US Constitution was ratified. It states:

> Neither slavery nor involuntary servitude, except as a punishment for crime whereof the party shall have been duly convicted, shall exist within the United States, or any place subject to their jurisdiction.[3]

Through this constitutional amendment, Congress made Taney's decision about slavery in the territories irrelevant. But the *Scott* decision relating to citizenship lingered. On July 9, 1868, the Fourteenth Amendment was ratified. It defines the qualifications for US citizenship, granting citizenship to former slaves. It reads:

> All persons born or naturalized in the United States, and subject to the jurisdiction thereof, are citizens

*of the United States and of the State wherein they reside. No State shall make or enforce any law which shall abridge the privileges or immunities of citizens of the United States; nor shall any State deprive any person of life, liberty, or property, without due process of law; nor deny to any person within its jurisdiction the equal protection of the laws.[4]*

Thus, 11 years after it was made, the majority opinion in the *Scott* case was nullified through two amendments to the US Constitution. ∼

# Chapter 11

# Dred Scott in History

The *Scott* decision is often cited as one of the worst decisions ever made by the Supreme Court, and Chief Justice Taney has taken much of the blame. Taney died on October 12, 1864, in the midst of the Civil War. At the time of his death, his home state of Maryland was taking steps to abolish slavery. Although Taney issued many important and influential decisions during his time as chief justice, it is the *Scott* decision that will forever be associated with his name.

## A CONTROVERSIAL SCULPTURE

Visitors to the Great Hall of the Supreme Court Building can see a row of busts of each of the chief justices. However, placing the bust of Chief Justice Taney in the hall was controversial when it was first suggested in 1865. Senator Charles Sumner of Massachusetts said, "I object to that; that now an emancipated country should make a bust to the author of the Dred Scott decision."[1] The Senate bill setting aside funds to erect a bust of Taney did not pass. In 1874, a congressional resolution allowed for the creation of such a bust, which was completed in 1877.

## The Supreme Court's Role

The controversial nature of the *Scott* decision has spurred many conversations among law experts, but one of the main discussions has revolved around the role of the Supreme Court. The Constitution establishes three branches of government with a system of checks and balances to keep each branch separate from the other. Some of the framers, such as Alexander Hamilton, believed the role of the Supreme Court was to protect the integrity of the Constitution, but this power is not explicitly mentioned in the document. This power was implied, however, and due to the constitutional structuring of the federal government, it became the role of the Supreme Court to hold Congress, the

People recognized the 150th anniversary of the *Scott* decision by placing pennies (representing Abraham Lincoln) on Scott's grave.

president, and state governments in check against the Constitution. In a process known as judicial review, the Supreme Court—which was intended to be impartial and unbiased—can declare an act of Congress or a decision of the president unconstitutional. Additionally, the doctrine of judicial supremacy holds that because the court is interpreting the Constitution, the highest law of the land, the court's decision is binding.

In the first few years of its existence, the Supreme Court issued few decisions, and it was viewed as the weakest of the three branches of government. But under Chief Justice John Marshall, the decision in *Marbury v. Madison* (1803) cemented the Supreme Court's ability to invalidate acts of Congress on the basis of unconstitutionality. The decision raised the status of the Supreme Court to the final interpreter of the Constitution. The Taney decision in the *Scott* case would continue in this tradition of the Supreme Court's power of judicial review.

But the judicial branch was also supposed to recognize when a case was so political in nature it could not be handled by the courts. Cases such as these called for judicial self-restraint. Taney himself said in 1838, "The powers given to the courts of the United States by the Constitution . . . are judicial powers and extend to those subjects only which are judicial in their character; and not to those which are political."[2] But time would reveal that, when provoked, the court under Taney would not hesitate to make a political decision.

When the *Scott* case made its way to the highest court in the nation, the US Supreme Court was held in high regard. But at the time, the justices were politically compromised. The majority of the justices were Democrats, and they felt the pressure of their proslavery party. Furthermore, Justice McLean was a contender for the Republican presidential nomination. After decades of debate and attempts at compromise over the issue of slavery, Congress passed the decision to the court. And Taney's court took the invitation, believing in its power of judicial supremacy to make a decisive ruling about issues that were threatening to tear apart the nation.

In the time since the decision, the court—and Taney in particular—have been denounced for their refusal to practice judicial self-restraint. After all, when the court ruled the case should have been thrown out for lack of jurisdiction, it could have stopped there. Justice Curtis, in his dissent, recognized this problem. According to Keith E. Whittington of Princeton University, Curtis knew "though involving important matters of political principle, the territory issue was a political question about which the Constitution did not provide adequate guidance for the courts. . . . It was an issue best resolved in the political arena."[3]

Did the court go too far in issuing its opinion? Should the court legislate from the bench? Was it an extreme decision in a case that should have been

## STEPHEN BREYER

In April 2010, Justice Stephen Breyer spoke about the *Scott* decision at the New York Historical Society. He spoke about politics and morality and stated:

> There is much to learn from this single historical example. Dred Scott teaches us the importance of solid reasoning, the dangers of reliance upon rhetoric, the need for practical constitutional interpretation consistent with our Nation's underlying values; and it teaches us the important role that morality and value play—or should play—at the intersection of law and politics. Dred Scott is thus one example that helps shed light on how courts can, and should, decide cases.[5]

rejected by the court because of its political nature? About the *Scott* decision, Justice Stephen Breyer said in October 2005, "If there's a lesson there, it's decide the case. Decide it. Don't try to do something that is going to save everybody. In fact, you might hurt everybody."[4]

By attempting to settle a political issue through a judicial decision, the Supreme Court did not quiet the problem as it intended. Instead, it added fuel to the fire. Therefore, in many ways, the legacy of the *Scott* decision is a legacy about the role of the Supreme Court overstepping its bounds. But there is no denying racial issues are a major part of that legacy as well.

## Dred Scott and Race Issues

Taney's *Scott* opinion declared outright that blacks could not be citizens and therefore did not have the rights constitutionally given to citizens of the United States. The passing of the Thirteenth, Fourteenth, and Fifteenth amendments in the years after the Civil War gave a new start to blacks in the United States.

But just because blacks had freedom and legal citizenship and black men had the right to vote did not mean they no longer suffered racism and injustice. The political implications of the *Scott* decision were overturned by subsequent legislation, but the ruling did a lot of damage, giving constitutional justification for a belief in the inferiority of blacks that would linger for decades. Indeed, in 1896, the Supreme Court ruling in *Plessy v. Ferguson* allowed legal segregation, a politically and socially supported policy that would endure until it was declared unconstitutional in 1954 in *Brown v. Board of Education of Topeka*.

Many believe that, for all its legal weight, the *Scott* legacy is truly one of racism, for the court's perceptions

*Left to right*: Lawyers George Hayes, Thurgood Marshall, and James Nabritt won their case in *Brown v. Board of Education*.

of the differences between whites and blacks significantly influenced its political decisions. Taney's majority opinion assumed a societal view of blacks as biologically, and therefore politically, inferior. Law professor Cecil J. Hunt argued that Taney's decision truly said blacks not only did not deserve citizenship, but they also did not deserve respect. Hunt believes this idea has lingered. Hunt writes,

> *One of the principal legacies of Dred Scott is the way these racial ideologies have insidiously sabotaged and undermined many of the national efforts to*

## ONE HUNDRED YEARS LATER

In 1957, Carl Brent Swisher of Johns Hopkins University discussed the *Scott* case and its connections to the Supreme Court's 1954 decision in *Brown v. Board of Education of Topeka*. Swisher wrote:

> *A vital assumption of our constitutional system is that we operate as a democracy. Leadership in constitutional development must come through the legislative and executive branches. . . . The judiciary can be the servant to democracy and a tremendous aid in the consolidation of democratic achievement, but it can never serve as a replacement of democracy itself.*[6]

## ISSUING AN APOLOGY

In 2008, the US House of Representatives formally apologized for slavery, and in 2009, the Senate did the same. Individual states, including Alabama, Florida, Maryland, New Jersey, North Carolina, and Virginia have also apologized for slavery. Law professor Alfred L. Brophy suggested the US Supreme Court and the Missouri courts should consider issuing an apology specifically for the *Dred Scott* decision. Brophy wrote:

> *In offering an apology, the courts would honor the memory of those who were enslaved. They would also acknowledge to Missouri and U.S. citizens that they understand that the sins of our country's past burden us still today. And they would help correct the ignorance of many Americans about our past.*[9]

However, as of 2012, neither court had issued an apology.

shake off the racial shackles of the past and achieve meaningful racial equality in America.[7]

Almost two centuries after *Scott*, the United States is still fraught with racial tensions, and African Americans face racism and discrimination. Therefore, the *Scott* decision contains lessons for today's society. According to Washington University Law professor David Konig, "The Dred Scott case isn't a ghost."[8] ～

# TIMELINE OF EVENTS AND RULINGS

| | | |
|---|---|---|
| 1820 | March | The Missouri Compromise prohibits slavery north of the 36° 30' parallel, with the exception of Missouri. |
| 1832 | June 23 | Dred Scott's owner Peter Blow dies; around this time Dr. John Emerson purchases Scott. |
| 1833 | December | Emerson and Scott travel to Fort Armstrong in Illinois. |
| 1836 | May | Emerson and Scott travel to Fort Snelling, near present-day Saint Paul, Minnesota. |
| 1837 | October | Emerson transfers to Saint Louis, Missouri, but Scott and his wife, Harriet, remain at Fort Snelling. |
| | November | Emerson moves to Fort Jesup in Louisiana. |
| 1838 | February 6 | Emerson marries Eliza Irene Sanford. Scott and Harriet travel to Louisiana soon after. |
| | October | Emerson, Irene, Scott, and Harriet travel back to Fort Snelling. |
| 1840 | May | Emerson, his wife, and the Scotts return to Saint Louis. |
| 1843 | December | Emerson dies. |
| 1846 | April 6 | Scott and Harriet file petitions to bring freedom suits against Irene Emerson. |
| 1847 | June 30 | The Scotts lose their case on a technicality. Scott's lawyers ask for a retrial. |

| | | |
|---|---|---|
| **1850** | **January 12** | The Saint Louis circuit court rules in favor of the Scotts, declaring them free. Emerson's lawyers appeal to the state supreme court. |
| **1852** | **March 22** | The Missouri Supreme Court overturns the lower court's decision, declaring the Scotts to be slaves. |
| **1853** | **November 2** | Scott begins a new suit in the US circuit court against John Sanford, the brother of Irene Emerson. |
| **1854** | **May 15** | Although it upholds Scott's right to sue in federal court, the court declares he is still a slave. Scott appeals to the US Supreme Court. |
| **1856** | **February 11** | The US Supreme Court begins hearing oral arguments in *Scott v. Sandford*. |
| | **December 15** | Reargument for *Scott v. Sandford* begins. |
| **1857** | **March 6** | Chief Justice Roger Taney delivers the majority opinion, declaring that Scott and his family are not free and blacks are not citizens. |
| | **May 26** | Taylor Blow emancipates the Scotts. |
| **1858** | **September 17** | Dred Scott dies. |
| **1865** | **December 6** | The Thirteenth Amendment abolishes slavery. |
| **1868** | **July 9** | The Fourteenth Amendment defines citizenship to include blacks who are born in the United States or naturalized. |
| **1870** | **February 3** | The Fifteenth Amendment gives black men the right to vote. |

# GLOSSARY

**abolition**

The act of ending slavery.

**confederation**

A league or alliance for mutual support, usually formed among states or nations.

**electoral vote**

A vote in the US Electoral College, which formally elects the US president and vice president.

**emancipate**

To set free.

**hypocrisy**

Pretending to believe something one does not believe.

**incumbent**

Someone who holds an office or position.

**indentured servant**

A person who sells himself into slavery for a defined period of time in order to acquire lodging or transport.

**insurrection**

Revolt against authority.

**militia**

A group of soldiers called to take up arms during emergencies.

**perpetuate**

To cause to continue.

**reversion**

A jurisdictional issue questioning whether the laws of a free state or a slave state should prevail when a slave returns to a slave state after being in a free state.

**secede**

To split away from the Union.

**slave codes**

Eighteenth and nineteenth-century laws governing slaves and the rights of slave owners that defined slaves as property, not people.

**sovereignty**

The right to self-government.

**territory**

A geographic area under US control that is not a part of an existing state.

# BRIEFS

## Petitioner

Dred Scott

## Respondent

John F. A. Sanford

## Date of Ruling

March 6, 1857

## Summary of Impacts

The owner of Dred Scott, a slave, took him to live in free
territories in the 1830s before returning to the slave state
of Missouri. In 1846, Scott sued his master's widow, Irene
Emerson, for his freedom. After Scott won his case in 1850
in the circuit court in Saint Louis, Emerson appealed to the
Missouri Supreme Court, which overturned the lower court's
decision in 1852 and declared Scott to be a slave. In 1854,
Scott began a new suit against John Sanford, Emerson's
brother, which was brought to the US circuit court. The circuit
court upheld Scott's right to sue but agreed with the Missouri
Supreme Court. Scott appealed to the US Supreme Court.

In 1857, Chief Justice Roger B. Taney delivered the 7–2
majority opinion, deciding Scott and his family were still
slaves. Furthermore, he declared Scott had no right to sue in
federal court. He went on to say blacks were not and could
not be citizens of the United States. Finally, he declared the
Missouri Compromise was unconstitutional and Congress
did not have the right to govern slavery in the territories. Two

justices, John McLean and Benjamin R. Curtis, dissented. After the Civil War, the Thirteenth Amendment to the US Constitution abolished slavery, and the Fourteenth Amendment defined citizenship to include blacks who are born in the United States or naturalized.

## Quotes

"The question before us is, whether the class of persons described in the plea in abatement [blacks] compose a portion of this people, and are constituent members of this sovereignty? We think they are not, and that they are not included, and were not intended to be included, under the word 'citizens' in the Constitution, and can therefore claim none of the rights and privileges which that instrument provides for and secures to citizens of the United States."

*—Chief Justice Roger Brooke Taney, in the majority decision, discussing US citizenship*

"I can find nothing in the Constitution which, . . . deprives of their citizenship any class of persons who were citizens of the United States at the time of its adoption, or who should be native-born citizens of any State after its adoption; nor any power enabling Congress to disfranchise persons born on the soil of any State, and entitled to citizenship of such State by its Constitution and laws."

*—Justice Benjamin R. Curtis, in a dissenting opinion*

# ADDITIONAL RESOURCES

## Selected Bibliography

Fehrenbacher, Don E. *The Dred Scott Case: Its Significance in American Law and Politics.* New York: Oxford UP, 1978. Print.

Finkelman, Paul. *Dred Scott v. Sandford: A Brief History with Documents.* Boston, MA: Bedford Books, 1997. Print.

Hopkins, Vincent C. *Dred Scott's Case.* New York: Russell & Russell, 1967. Print.

Stampp, Kenneth M. *America in 1857: A Nation on the Brink.* New York: Oxford UP: 1981. Print.

## Further Readings

*Abraham Lincoln, Slavery, and the Civil War: Selected Writings and Speeches.* Michael P. Johnson, ed. Boston, MA: Bedford/St. Martin's, 2011. Print.

Baum, Lawrence. *The Supreme Court.* 10th ed. Washington DC: CQ Press, 2010. Print.

Maltz, Earl M. *Dred Scott and the Politics of Slavery.* Lawrence, KS: UP of Kansas, 2007. Print.

## Web Links

To learn more about *Dred Scott v. Sandford*, visit ABDO Publishing Company online at **www.abdopublishing.com**. Web sites about *Scott* are featured on our Book Links page. These links are routinely monitored and updated to provide the most current information available.

## Places to Visit

**Dred Scott's Quarters at Historic Fort Snelling**
200 Tower Avenue, Saint Paul, MN 55111
612-726-1171
http://www.historicfortsnelling.org/plan-visit/what-do/dred-scotts-quarters
At Fort Snelling, Dred Scott met and married Harriet Robinson. Visit the site and see the building where Dred and Harriet Scott likely lived.

**Old Courthouse at Jefferson National Expansion Memorial**
11 North Fourth Street, Saint Louis, Missouri 63102
314-655-1700
http://www.nps.gov/jeff/index.htm
Visit the courthouse that hosted the first two trials of the *Dred Scott* case.

**The Supreme Court Building**
1 First Street, NE, Washington, DC 20543
202-479-3000
http://www.supremecourt.gov/Default.aspx
At the Supreme Court Building, visitors can sit in on oral arguments, attend lectures, tour the building, see exhibitions, and view statues of the chief justices.

# SOURCE NOTES

## Chapter 1. The Decision Announced

1. "Important Slave Case." *The New York Times.* The New York Times, 16 Dec. 1856. Web. 1 June 2011.

2. *Inaugural Addresses of the Presidents of the United States, Volume 1: George Washington (1789) to James A. Garfield (1881).* Bedford, MA: Applewood Books, 2000. *Google Books.* Web. 116.

3. Vincent C. Hopkins. *Dred Scott's Case.* New York: Fordham UP, 1951. Print. 38.

## Chapter 2. Slavery in the New World

1. Lerone Bennett. *The Shaping of Black America.* New York: Penguin, 1993. Print. 16.

2. James Oliver Horton and Lois E. Horton. *Slavery and the Making of America.* New York: Oxford UP, 2005. Print. 25–26.

3. James Oliver Horton and Lois E. Horton. *Slavery and the Making of America.* New York: Oxford UP, 2005. Print. 31.

4. Don E. Fehrenbacher. *The Dred Scott Case: Its Significance in American Law and Politics.* New York: Oxford UP, 1978. Print. 15–16.

5. "Declaration of Independence." *Charters of Freedom.* National Archives and Records Administration, n.d. Web. 16 July 2011.

6. James Oliver Horton and Lois E. Horton. *Slavery and the Making of America.* New York: Oxford UP, 2005. Print. 61–63.

7. Don E. Fehrenbacher. *The Dred Scott Case: Its Significance in American Law and Politics.* New York: Oxford UP, 1978. Print. 17.

8. James Oliver Horton and Lois E. Horton. *Slavery and the Making of America.* New York: Oxford UP, 2005. Print. 51.

9. "United States Constitution: Article I." *Cornell University Law School.* Cornell University Law School, n.d. Web. 16 July 2011.

10. "United States Constitution: Article IV." *Cornell University Law School.* Cornell University Law School, n.d. Web. 16 July 2011.

## Chapter 3. The Territorial Question

1. Dethloff, Henry C. "Louisiana Purchase." *World Book Advanced*. World Book, 2011. Web. 28 June 2011.

2. "Free Soil Party." *Ohio History Central*. Ohio Historical Society, 1 July 2005. Web. 16 July 2011.

## Chapter 4. Slaves, Freedom, and Civil Rights

1. Michael Trotti. "Freedmen and Enslaved Soil: A Case Study of Manumission, Migration, and Land." *The Virginia Magazine of History and Biography* 104.4 (Autumn 1996): 455–480. *JSTOR*. Web. 16 July 2011. 458.

2. "Constitution of the United States." *Charters of Freedom*. National Archives and Records Administration, n.d. Web. 16 July 2011.

3. "The Meaning of July 4th for the Negro." *Africans in America*. WGBH/PBS Online, n.d. Web. 16 July 2011.

4. Don E. Fehrenbacher. *The Dred Scott Case: Its Significance in American Law and Politics*. New York: Oxford UP, 1978. Print. 70.

**Chapter 5. Who Was Dred Scott?**
1. Walter Ehrlich. *They Have No Rights: Dred Scott's Struggle for Freedom*. Bedford, MA: Applewood Books, 1979. *Google Book Search*. Web. 12 Mar. 2012.
2. Carl Brent Swisher. "Dred Scott One Hundred Years After." *The Journal of Politics* 19.2 (May 1957): 167–183. *JSTOR*. Web. 16 July 2011. 167.
3. Paul Finkelman. *Dred Scott v. Sandford: A Brief History with Documents*. Boston, MA: Bedford Books, 1997. Print. 15.
4. "Slavery at Fort Snelling (1820s–1850s)." *Historic Fort Snelling*. Web. Minnesota Historical Society, 2012. Web. 12 Mar. 2012.
5. Don E. Fehrenbacher. *The Dred Scott Case: Its Significance in American Law and Politics*. New York: Oxford UP, 1978. Print. 244.
6. "Missouri's Dred Scott Case." *Missouri Digital Heritage*. Missouri State Archives, n.d. Web. 16 July 2011.

**Chapter 6. *Scott v. Emerson***
1. "Motion for New Trial (in Dred Scott Case)." *Dred Scott Case Collection*. Washington University Libraries, n.d. Web. 16 July 2011.
2. Paul Finkelman. *Dred Scott v. Sandford: A Brief History with Documents*. Boston, MA: Bedford Books, 1997. Print. 22.

## Chapter 7. The Case against Sanford

1. "DRED SCOTT v. SANDFORD, 60 U.S. 393 (1856)." *FindLaw.* FindLaw, n.d. Web. 16 July 2011.

2. Don E. Fehrenbacher. *The Dred Scott Case: Its Significance in American Law and Politics.* New York: Oxford UP, 1978. Print. 280.

3. Vincent C. Hopkins. *Dred Scott's Case.* New York: Fordham UP, 1951. Print. 25.

## Chapter 8. Before the Supreme Court

1. Vincent C. Hopkins. *Dred Scott's Case.* New York: Fordham UP, 1951. Print. 34.

2. Ibid. 35.

3. "A Century of Lawmaking for a New Nation: U.S. Congressional Documents and Debates, 1774–1875, Statutes at Large, 16th Congress, 1st Session." *The Library of Congress.* The Library of Congress, n.d. Web. 16 July 2011.

4. "Constitution of the United States." *Charters of Freedom.* National Archives and Records Administration, n.d. Web. 16 July 2011.

5. "DRED SCOTT v. SANDFORD, 60 U.S. 393 (1856)." *FindLaw.* FindLaw, n.d. Web. 16 July 2011.

6. Ibid.

7. Ibid.

8. Ibid.

9. Ibid.

10. Ibid.

## Chapter 9. The Conclusions Reached

1. "David Blight on the Dred Scott decision." *Africans in America*. WGBH/PBS Online, n.d. Web. 16 July 2011.

2. Paul Finkelman. *Dred Scott v. Sandford: A Brief History with Documents*. Boston, MA: Bedford Books, 1997. Print. 145.

3. Ibid. 149.

4. Ibid. 134.

5. "DRED SCOTT v. SANDFORD, 60 U.S. 393 (1856)." *FindLaw*. FindLaw, n.d. Web. 16 July 2011.

6. Don E. Fehrenbacher. *The Dred Scott Case: Its Significance in American Law and Politics*. New York: Oxford UP, 1978. Print. 425.

7. "The Dred Scott Decision." *New York Times*. New York Times, 15 Aug. 1857. Web. 16 July 2011.

8. Don E. Fehrenbacher. *The Dred Scott Case: Its Significance in American Law and Politics*. New York: Oxford UP, 1978. Print. 447.

## Chapter 10. Amending the Constitution

1. "Dred Scott." *New York Times*. New York Times, 21 Sept. 1858. Web. 16 July 2011.

2. "Lincoln's 'House Divided' Speech." *Africans in America*. WGBH/PBS Online, n.d. Web. 16 July 2011.

3. "Constitution of the United States: Amendments 11–27." *Charters of Freedom*. National Archives and Records Administration, n.d. Web. 16 July 2011.

4. Ibid.

5. Ibid.

## Chapter 11. Dred Scott in History

1. "Roger B. Taney." *United States Senate*. www.senate.gov, n.d. Web. 17 July 2011.

2. Don E. Fehrenbacher. *The Dred Scott Case: Its Significance in American Law and Politics*. New York: Oxford UP, 1978. Print. 230.

3. Keith E. Whittington. "The Road Not Taken: Dred Scott, Judicial Authority, and Political Questions." *The Journal of Politics* 63.2 (May 2001): 365–391. *JSTOR*. Web. 16 July 2011. 367.

4. "150th Anniversary of the Dred Scott Decision." *C-SPAN Video Library*. C-SPAN, 8 Mar. 2007. Web. 16 July 2011.

5. "Justice Breyer on the Dred Scott Decision." *The Defenders Online*. The Defenders Online, 28 May 2010. Web. 17 July 2011.

6. Carl Brent Swisher. "Dred Scott One Hundred Years After." *The Journal of Politics* 19.2 (May 1957): 167–183. *JSTOR*. Web. 16 July 2011. 183.

7. Cecil J. Hunt, II. "No Right to Respect: Dred Scott and the Southern Honor Culture." *New England Law Review* 42 (Fall 2007): 79–108. *HeinOnline*. Web. 81–82.

8. Konig, David Thomas, Paul Finkelman, and Christopher Alan Bracey, Eds. *The Dred Scott Case: Historical and Contemporary Perspectives on Race and Law*. Athens, OH: Ohio UP, 2010. *Google Books*. 186.

9. "Dred Scott Legacy; Stereotypes Still Felt in the Courts." *Newswise*. Newswise, Inc, 20 Apr. 2007. Web. 17 July 2011.

# INDEX

## A

abolitionists, 20, 30, 43, 49, 80, 89, 113, 115

American Civil War, 17, 49, 80, 124–126, 128, 130, 136

*Amy v. Smith*, 93

## B

Bay, Samuel Mansfield, 73, 76

Birch, James H., 75

Blair, Montgomery, 15, 89, 92–93, 95–99, 101, 115

Bleeding Kansas, 13, 92

Blow, Peter, 60–61

Blow, Taylor, 71, 120

Blow family, 63, 71, 85

Breyer, Stephen, 135

*Brown v. Board of Education of Topeka*, 136, 138

Buchanan, James, 14–15, 96, 113, 121, 123

## C

Campbell, John A., 93, 97, 106, 124

Catron, John, 93, 97, 106

Chaffee, Calvin C., 115, 120

Cheever, George B., 115

citizenship, 11, 29, 58–59, 86–87, 90, 93, 95, 96, 97–98, 101–102, 106–108, 110–111, 128–129, 136, 138

Compromise of 1850, 79, 80

Constitutional Convention, 28–32, 34, 37, 46, 108, 119

Curtis, Benjamin R., 93, 97, 101, 103, 106–108, 113, 116, 124, 134

Curtis, George T., 97

## About the Author

Amy Van Zee is an editor and writer who lives near Minneapolis, Minnesota. She has an English degree from the University of Minnesota and has contributed to dozens of educational books.

## About the Content Consultant

Professor Maltz is the author of *Rethinking Constitutional Law: Originalism, Interventionism, and the Politics of Judicial Review*; *Civil Rights, the Constitution, and Congress, 1863–1865*; and more than 50 articles.

Per RFP 03764 Follett School Solutions guarantees
hardcover bindings through SY 2024-2025
877.899.8550 or customerservice@follett.com